The Diary of an Ad Man

THE

Diary of an Ad Man

THE WAR YEARS
JUNE 1, 1942 – DECEMBER 31, 1943

James Webb Young

ADVERTISING PUBLICATIONS, INC.
CHICAGO, ILL.

Printed in the U. S. A.
ADVERTISING PUBLICATIONS, INC.
CHICAGO

To
E. J. Y.
who
has lived
through it

Foreword

This book came about more or less by accident. In the spring of 1942, while lunching one day with George Crain in Chicago, I began telling him about a book I wanted to write on a certain period of American business history, as seen from an advertising man's point of view.

I was on my way west, to my ranch in New Mexico; and George urged me to get at this writing there, doing it first in weekly installments for *Advertising Age*. Well knowing the power of closing dates as a taskmaster, I thought this a good idea.

A few weeks later I began a routine of making daily notes for such a book, but found myself handicapped by the lack of historical reference material. As a result, these daily notes began to take on, more and more, a current flavor; and this led eventually to the idea of the Diary as a way to appease George's importunities for the promised material.

The Diary ran in *Advertising Age* anonymously because I felt that would give me more freedom of expression, and involve me in less labor over controversial subjects. Also, because I had a sly notion that this would get it more word-of-mouth advertising from the curious — as it did.

But some friends saw through this anonymity from the start, in spite of occasional entries deliberately designed to cover my trail, by placing incidents in times and places other than those where they happened.

So much of the material has seemed to me to be of a topical and ephemeral nature that I have been surprised at the demand for a book to be made of it. But some of you asked for it, so here it is, with my appreciation for yours. I have had a lot of fun doing it, wholly because it discovered for me so many people sympathetic to some of my own ideas about this activity we call advertising. And because it has seemed to demonstrate again my particular belief that words gain wings in proportion as they are allowed to express a personality.

My special thanks are due to my friend Paul Berdanier, who designed the format and typography for this book. Incidentally, it was he who thought the title page should carry my ranch brand, Bar Nuthin'.

J. W. Y.

June, 1942

Monday . . . June 1

Talked with a New Deal newspaper man, now high up in the councils of the Coordinator of Information. Asked him why they had not made more use of advertising men. He said he had come to the conclusion that some of them could be "converted" to the New Deal and thus made useful. Have long suspected that this was an attitude of many of the more rabid brethren in Washington, but never met one brazen enough to say it before. Close to treason.

Tuesday . . . June 2

Spent the evening reading the latest issue of the quarterly *Print*. Both mechanically and editorially this is the best job that has ever been done in the graphic arts field. Any man whose early dreams were compounded of Caslon Old Style and printer's ink will give it a permanent place on his shelves.

Wednesday . . . June 3

Developed a new headline for one of my mail order accounts, which ought to be a whiz. But will

11

it? The key sheets will tell. Funny how much harder one works on a headline when it has this kind of check. But I have seen a change of just one phrase in a headline change results as much as 50%.

Thursday . . . June 4

Asked a wise old Catholic priest friend of mine how anybody could believe in the doctrine of the Trinity. His answer: "By preaching it." Guess that's how ad men come to believe in the products they sell. Might be something for my New Deal friend, above, to consider. Always thought the only difference between ad men and preachers was a sense of direction. In fact, once discovered in a theological school a course called "homiletics" which deals with the same techniques of persuasion which ad men use.

Friday . . . June 5

Visited a bigger and better Super Market, which has just been opened on the outskirts. Wonderful layout, including a Beauty Shoppe, Lending Library, and Post Office Station. Big parking lot, with six cars on it, but more people than that inside. Good observation post to see how people buy food. Some reach straight and quick for the brand they want. Others look them all over and compare prices. This varies with types of products. But, Lord, what an exhibit the whole place makes of the high standard of American living. We don't know our wealth.

12

Saturday . . . June 6

Reread that piece of MacArthur's about the fall of Corregidor. Wonderful copy, written with passion, as good copy ought to be. Thank God this General seems to be equally good with words and deeds.

Sunday . . . June 7

Worked in the garden, and thought about how constant cultivation is needed to keep all kinds of plants healthy— both horticultural and industrial.

Monday . . . June 8

On the train to Los Angeles met a southern California manufacturer of women's sports wear. He buys textiles in the East, ships them to the coast, cuts and sews them, and ships many of the garments back east again. Asked him whether low wages for coast workers made this possible. He said, No, nothing but the style ideas and glamor of California turned the trick. Now, however, he is producing practically nothing but snappy slacks and other garments for women defense workers. Takes sports wear experience to cut a pair of pants which women will wear and can work in, he claimed.

Tuesday . . . June 9

Went to a rehearsal for a big radio show in Hollywood, starring Norma Shearer. Didn't catch her name on the introduction, but thought her chestnut hair so beautiful asked later who she was. Stared at like a man from Mars. Show business, the Brown Derby, and Crossley ratings are the whole of advertising to these people.

Wednesday . . . June 10

Coming back on the train met another California garment manufacturer, who had done a little advertising in national magazines. Coast people combine a peculiar local pride with an itch for national recognition. He used an agency I never heard of, and complained that they did nothing for their commission. Later it developed that this "agency" was really the representative of a small trade paper, and that a cut rate in the trade paper had offset the magazine commissions. Asked him how he expected any service from such a setup.

Thursday . . . June 11

Talked with a publisher whose advertising volume is down about 25 per cent so far this year, with costs up. A serious problem for him; but reader response to an increased subscription rate encourages him. Believe the economics of publishing rested too much on advertising revenue in the past, and that this forced shift to more revenue from the reader will make a healthier structure in the future.

14

Friday . . . June 12

Received from England two copies of one of their oldest and best rural life magazines. Still carrying a surprising amount of advertising. Much in it about the necessity for that country to do more to feed itself, including open advocacy of nationalization of farm land as a solution. Surprising people, the English. We think of them as ultra conservative, yet they have already adopted many "schemes," as they call them, which would elsewhere be called socialism.

Saturday . . . June 13

At the farm, deciding whether to sell pigs now or feed them through. Advertising operates to such a large extent within a fixed price structure that most of us don't know much about price risks. Farming a quick means to such an education.

Sunday . . . June 14

My daughter showing signs of interest in the business. Asked me today what I thought about women in advertising. Told her I didn't think anything about them—was only interested in whether a person, man or woman, had advertising talent. She wanted to know whether the woman's point of view wasn't valuable in itself. Pointed out that —old wives' tales to the contrary—there were plenty of men who understood women—and made their living by predicting what women would do.

15

Monday . . . *June 15*

A new account in the house today put a spring in every step and a gleam in every eye. The anti-pellagra vitamin of the ad business. This one especially so, because it has implications for the brave, new world which optimists again predict for the post-war period. Even an ad man has yearnings to play his part in that world, and to feel that he, too, has social significance.

Tuesday . . . *June 16*

Went through a copy of *Life*, testing each ad to see how many offered anything I was in the market for or would by any possibility be interested in buying. Found only three, and those small ones in the back of the book. Makes the general run of low reading ratings by Starch *et al.* understandable. But actual buying by only one-tenth of one per cent of a circulation will often make an ad profitable, as the records of direct sales copy will show.

Wednesday . . . *June 17*

A publication salesman who called on me today listened politely every time I tried to explain why his proposition did not fit a client's needs. But he never picked up or argued a single point I made. All he did was to keep reaching for more evidence of how his book had paid somebody else, and keep pounding that home. Not a bad method.

16

Thursday . . . June 18

Surprised at the number of people of my acquaintance, outside the business, who have commented on the change in the *S. E. P.* Most did not seem to like it. As near as I could make out, they felt the loss of the old personality and a not quite clear definition of a new one. Probably that will evolve.

Friday . . . June 19

Wrote a pattern piece of copy that pleased me and the client. That still adds up as a day in which something real was accomplished. Why do so many of us who made our way in this business as copy writers quit writing?

Saturday . . . June 20

Visited with an old country woman, over seventy, who praised the Lord and blessed His Name. For the first time in her life she has running water in her house. It's just a cold water spigot in her kitchen sink, with another outside for her flowers, but it means no more toting from the old well. Riches.

Sunday . . . June 21

Riding horseback along a country lane I saw wild roses in bloom, against an old stone wall. The expensive, improved varieties in my garden have lost something. Sophistication always does.

17

Monday . . . *June 22*

See by the papers that S.M., who used to write darn good copy for me, has two new accounts. When I saw him on the Century a few weeks ago he was feeling the pinch of priorities. But I'll stay in business, he said, if it's only with one room and a sign reading "Ads Made Here." Such men have an inner assurance about their ability to put selling words on paper which always carries them through.

Tuesday . . . *June 23*

What's all this pother about whether the government should advertise? It already is advertising, extensively. Those sensible professional fellows who run the Army and Navy make no bones about it, and seem to have no difficulties over it—either with publishers left off the list or with their Congressmen. The other administrators will learn in due time that the old Biblical saw about "line upon line, precept upon precept" is still true, and that paid advertising is the only form of mass communication which supplies it.

Wednesday . . . *June 24*

Up early, feeding the plants in my garden Vigoro. Wondered why this product was the only case I could think of where any one of the big packers had pioneered a new market.

18

Thursday . . . June 25

At lunch today on the Tavern terrace listened again to that perennial debate over the relative importance of creative men and account executives in agencies. The creative men claim too much. A garden must have plenty of fertilizer if plants are to flourish, but even so grasshoppers can do you out of fruit or bloom. Creative men usually supply the chemicals that make accounts grow, but, Lord, how the grasshoppers need to be watched!

Friday . . . June 26

A woman correspondent thinks I don't have a proper appreciation of her sex in advertising. Apparently because I didn't rate women as making a unique contribution. An even break is not enough. Reminds me of the time a charming lady told me, at length, how much more practical women were than men. I admitted it, and said that men, of course, were the idealistic sex. But this didn't suit her at all; she wanted women granted priorities to both.

Saturday . . . June 27

Forty hours a week may be wrong in war time, but I would hate to lose those quiet Saturday mornings at the office. There is nothing so moral as a cleaned up desk at the week-end.

19

Sunday . . . June 28

Tried my hand at writing a folder for a scientific institution which badly needs new supporting members. Wanted to see if I could get through the insulation of scientific verbiage, and make their story interesting, intelligible, and important to the average man. Pleased with myself.

Monday . . . June 29

Showed my attempt at popularizing science to a newspaper writer. He said it still had too many five dollar words, and wanted to know why I couldn't put it into hotel English. In fact, treated me pretty roughly, and said he supposed if I wanted to describe a fellow as a poor business man I would say he was "inept in monetary matters."

Tuesday . . . June 30

Spent a couple of hours with drawing board, T-square, and colored pencils, working over some art department rough layouts which didn't please me. Understand the progressive pedagogues now say that every child could be taught to draw just as easily as he is taught to write. Would to heaven such a notion had been held in my school days. The ad maker needs the facility to express himself in pictures as well as words, and if I were a young copywriter again I would get a drawing teacher.

July, 1942

Wednesday . . . July 1

W. L. is, perhaps, more deft at writing certain kinds of copy than any other man I know. He has a simplicity and a niceness in the choice of words which makes a piece of his text as clearcut as a cameo. He was raised on this kind of printed advertising, yet he has become equally good at daytime radio, and is the author of one of our most successful soap operas. If his career had been in the Navy, and he had been raised on a battleship, he would have been among the first to learn to fly.

Thursday . . . July 2

Talked with a Washington Big Shot who has seen some of the leading ad men there perform. When I asked what he thought of them he said he was amazed at their illiteracy. Clever fellows at their trade, he said, but woefully lacking in understanding of world affairs, political forces, and international economics such as the times call for. Ouch!

21

Friday . . . July 3

Read with regret for the *Reader's Digest* its attack on cigaret advertising. A performance unworthy of this fine publication. Based on inadequate testing, as any one knows who has made such variable experiments. This inadequate evidence then used to cast an air of scientific validity over such prejudice words as "coffin nails." The underlying W.C.T.U. determination is revealed by treatment of Old Golds. This brand makes the best showing in the *Digest's* own test for nicotine and throat irritants, yet makes no claims of this kind. Instead, it sticks to flavor, which the *Digest* says is the only basis for cigaret difference. But does this win applause? Not at all—only criticism for not stating the quantity of flavorful leaf employed.

Saturday . . . July 4

Prodded by my wife, after a fried chicken dinner, to go get the last of the late sweet cherries, in the top of the tree. Like doing the trade paper ads in a campaign, picking is slower in these topmost branches, so they are always put off to the last. But often the plumpest and sweetest cherries are there.

Sunday . . . July 5

Skimming through Cardinal Newman's great book, "Apologia Pro Vita Sua" I was led to cogitate

22

on the apology for an ad man's life. If it is to have any permanent meaning, I thought, it must be aimed in the long run at reducing the costs of distribution, so that more people can get more and more goods for less and less.

Monday . . . July 6

Lord! how tired I am of all this tendency to ballyhoo the war. Magazine editors, newspaper columnists, radio commentators, and Washington headline hunters all seem determined to dramatize it and jazz it up. They act like press agents for a "Roosevelt & Hopkins' Greatest Show on Earth." It is true that for awhile we had ringside seats at history. But now we are in the ring, with a serious, dirty, and dangerous job to do. We ought to cut out the showmanship and get on with it.

Tuesday . . . July 7

The advertising manager for one of our clients telephoned a hurry-up call today for an agate rule. Seems that his Big Boss had suddenly heard of agate lines, and wanted to measure one of his newspaper ads with such a rule. The A.M. was embarrassed not to have one in the house. It used to be that every ad man, like a good workman, carried an agate rule in his vest pocket. But nowadays one is hardly ever seen outside an art or mechanical department.

23

Wednesday . . . July 8

Succeeded today in digging up a romantic bit of history which will add color to one of our products. It is not sufficiently recognized—especially by the critics of advertising—that romance in its broad sense is the most wanted product in the world. So many people lead lives of "quiet desperation" that any advertising which offers them escape, and any product which offers them utility plus color, performs a profound service.

Thursday . . . July 9

A letter from an advertising friend in England tells how they have been forced there to make use of smaller spaces in newspapers. He speaks of having to learn all over again to make small space effective, and suggests that we may have to do the same thing here. With no shortage of newsprint yet, such as there is in England, we may not come to it. But it is true that our creators of advertising today either never had, or have largely lost, the art of making small space pay.

Friday . . . July 10

A young man in high school wants to know how he can begin now to prepare himself for a job in advertising after the war. In particular he asks, What are the best books about advertising? Told him I held with J. Y., who says somewhere that

24

the best books about advertising are not about advertising. Meaning, of course, that advertising is a subject as broad as life itself; and that it is better to read broadly for an understanding of life, rather than narrowly for an understanding of advertising.

Saturday . . . July 11

Spent the morning picking apricots, whose lovely color makes them the pleasantest of all fruits to handle. Wished again that our civilization could be so organized that every man could have some such outdoor work part of every day. There is mental as well as physical health in it.

Sunday . . . July 12

Spent a twilight hour sitting on the fence watching my pigs make hogs of themselves. If pork prices hold until fall I may even come to feel kindly toward the farm bloc in Congress.

Monday . . . July 13

What's happened to our analogy boys? So far I haven't seen a single piece of advertising literature which promotes a campaign as a "task force."

Tuesday . . . July 14

No industry has had a greater stake in the private enterprise system than advertising. From the *en-*

trepreneur all our blessings have flowed. His imagination for a new consumer service, his capital and the courage to risk it, have been the springs of our business. Now there begins to be, even in high business quarters, an acceptance of the idea that the era of private enterprise is past. Advertising people need to subject this idea to the most critical scrutiny; and to set themselves to expose whatever fallacies are in it. A recent report to the Twentieth Century Fund by Stuart Chase, called "The Road We Are Traveling," makes a good case for this idea, and is a good place to start an examination of it.

Wednesday . . . July 15

How much more workmanlike our copywriters would be if they had learned to stick type in their youth. No writer can see his ad "whole," or plan its total impact, without visualizing the type face and its setting. Also, learning to scale his writing to his type is an art every writer should be forced to practice. Note how neatly newspaper headline writers and *Life's* caption writers do it. With a book like Lopatecki's "Typographer's Desk Manual," anybody with any feel for type can keep printers from going mad.

Thursday . . . July 16

Talked with one of the elder statesmen of advertising about the post-war world and the future of our private enterprise system. He said he couldn't worry too much about it, believing that under any kind of system persuasion would be needed, and that there would be some place for the man who had made an art of it.

Friday . . . July 17

In the beginning of communication there was sound; a noise that came to stand for "Look out!" or "Come here!" Then there were pictures which came to stand for things and action—hieroglyphics. Then the pictures became signs for the sounds which could be put together to make words. So all sounds, pictures, and written words have the same purpose, namely, to stand as symbols for other things. We can speak, draw, or write "cow" and it flashes the cow-thing to our minds. Some symbols are more vivid as sounds (moo cow); some more vivid as pictures (red cow); some more vivid in print (sacred cow). The ad man, whose business is communication for purposes of persuasion, should aim at being equally adept with all kinds of symbols.

Saturday . . . July 18

Went to a reception and exhibit for a well-known portrait painter, who has done such tycoons and celebrities as Roy Howard, Thomas Watson, Arthur Brisbane, etc. A man who has never done advertising illustrations, but would be good for any calling for strong masculine portraiture.

Sunday . . . July 19

Some of my farm neighbors have a real gift for the picturesque phrase. Talking with one today he said of another neighbor that he was the kind of fellow who was so lucky "he could fall down a well and come up with his pockets full of fish."

Monday . . . July 20

A successful woman in one of our top flight agencies writes me to tell my aspiring daughter that "my father, too, was in the advertising business; I followed right along after him, have earned a respectable living, and had a marvelous life!" Daughter, being told, vows that she will go and do likewise. Guess I will have to look about for a friendly competitor to take her in. A man should no more try to teach his daughter advertising than teach his wife to drive—which remark, I suppose, dates me.

Tuesday . . . July 21

Visited with a grocery jobber in a distributing town of 20,000 population. He took me through his warehouse to show me the gaps in his stock. Item after item was either completely gone or about to be, with no more in sight. It made a picture which foreshadows the consumer pinch about to come.

Wednesday . . . July 22

The president of one of our client companies came to me today to make serious complaint about the service we are giving them. The net of the matter was that we were not contributing enough in basic thinking and planning, and in imaginative development work on the account, and he was right. I decided that I would have to tell him why; namely, that he had put between us and his organization an advertising manager whose caliber was too small—so that even when we had a four-inch flow at our end only a two-inch stream got piped in to him.

Thursday . . . July 23

Musing further on my daughter's desire to enter the business, I asked myself what I really believed was the best training for a beginner. How would I try to get started if I were young again, with no experience and no assets to offer except a general education? Decided I would do it as a stenographer, whether I were boy or girl. That would not only give me something tangible to sell to an employer, but would put me in a job where I could see the wheels go round and get a sense of what the business is all about. From that I would move on to training in the specific techniques of the business.

Friday . . . July 24

Shopping around a large "fancy" grocery store, with its own bakery, I noticed that not a single loaf on the bread rack had the word Enriched on it. And this was in a store patronized by what might be thought to be the most intelligent part of the population. When I asked the grocer why this lack his laconic answer was: "No demand."

Saturday . . . July 25

Under government pressure a tremendous amount of food advertising is now bearing down heavily on nutrition. That there has been some increase in the public interest in this subject I do not doubt. But let's don't fool ourselves: what we *ought* to eat is still less interesting than what we *want* to eat. When the great mass of women answer the thrice-daily question, What shall we have to eat? it is quite likely to be in terms of what the family likes.

Sunday . . . July 26

Having written the above last night, picked my blackberries this morning, and did heavy justice to them in a pie for Sunday dinner.

Monday . . . July 27

I have named our new receptionist Miss Malaprop. When I asked her this morning how she liked her job, she said it was fine; the gentlemen from the publications told her such funny antidotes.

Tuesday . . . July 28

Great argument with an art director over pictures versus words. The success of *Life* seemed to him to settle the question for all time. Called his attention to the equal or greater success of the *Reader's Digest*, practically without a picture in it. Apparently *what* you say is still more important than *how* you say it.

Wednesday . . . July 29

A large general advertiser, having seen a piece of my copy for a mail order advertiser, wanted to know why he couldn't get the same intimate, personal tone in his. I told him he could if (1) he would waive his insistence on short copy; (2) let me use or create an individual to speak for his corporation; (3) let this individual talk colloquially, direct to the reader. The success of radio as an advertising medium may be attributed very largely to the observance of these three points in many commercials.

Thursday . . . July 30

A relatively new building supply dealer in our suburban area has been advertising consistently in the local paper. His ads have been small, but inter-

31

esting. They made me conscious of his existence, but brought me no occasion to switch my patronage from his long-established competitor. Then my wife saw an ad in a national magazine for a new kind of awning paint, and answered its invitation to write for color cards, etc. With these came the information that the aforesaid advertising dealer carried the product. Then the dealer wrote, saying our inquiry had come to him. My wife asked if I had ever heard of him and I said yes. So in we went, bought two quarts of paint, plus 12 boxes of kalsomine on which he had a sale, two garden gadgets, and a rake which we remembered needing. Yet some folks wonder *how* advertising pays.

Friday . . . July 31

Writing down the above made me remember a note book which I used to carry when I first started advertising work, too many years ago. After some search I found it. In it I had put down an account, such as the above, of every observation I could make as to how advertising had started a sale. Some were from my own experiences; others were acquired by questioning friends; and still others by inducing customers to talk in a retail store where I helped out on Saturday afternoons. Altogether I accumulated over a hundred case histories of this kind, and I believe I learned more about advertising from them than from anything else I ever did.

32

August, 1942

Saturday . . . August 1

Visited with a country storekeeper, who also has a gas pump. A big car, chauffeur-driven, came up, and the dealer being busy elsewhere I filled the tank. When the lady in back paid me she graciously added a quarter tip. First clear profit for my farm overalls!

Sunday . . . August 2

Finished reading Jane Austen's novel, "Sense and Sensibility." Because Mark Twain said that a good library was one which contained none of her works, I had always scorned the reading of them. But this one, at least, is an excellent study of character, as valid today as when it was first published in 1812. A great picture, too, of that genteel England which set so many of the patterns for the England of today. Helpful to get this, with Anglo-American understanding becoming increasingly important in our lives.

Monday . . . August 3

God bless Miss Malaprop! I can see that she is

going to add color to my life. Today I asked what her friends thought about her working in the advertising business—did any of them think it was a racket? Why, no, she said; she had never heard of any stamina attached to this business. Stigma?

Tuesday . . . August 4

The boys who are helping the Advertising Council prepare campaigns for government purposes are making a mistake. They are using too many of the conventional tricks of the trade in their copy. The public is in no mood for this when it comes to war aims. All they want and need is to be told simply, clearly, and authoritatively what they should do— and Lord! how they want that. The less like advertising the message is, the better the results will be.

Wednesday . . . August 5

So many people have now left our organization for the various services that those who remain are beginning to complain of overwork. I tell them that if they had ever thinned vegetables in a garden they would know this just gives them more room to grow.

Thursday . . . August 6

As every organization grows and gets older it accumulates its mistakes and deadwood in personnel. There isn't any doubt that some of our people

34

who have left for war service would have had to be let go, sooner or later, anyhow. So what do we do when these people begin to come home and want their jobs back? This is one kind of post-war planning every manager can begin to do now.

Friday . . . August 7

An out-of-town acquaintance who runs a specialty shop, selling rather high priced, unique home furnishings, asked me today for some advice about the kind of advertising he should do. He has spent, for him, quite a little money in magazine ads, and never made one of them pay. Similar shops with similar merchandise have made magazine and newspaper advertising pay when located in a big city, where their advertising could build customers and good will as well as make immediate sales. But my friend is not so located, and he will never pay out on a mail order basis. There is still too high a mortality among small first year advertisers of this kind, because from neither agents nor media representatives can they get the kind of guidance they need.

Saturday . . . August 8

Speaking of failures reminds me of the time I tried, as chairman of a program committee, to get two of our leading agents to tell the stories of their first advertising failures. Could I do it? Any program chairman who wants to try is welcome to the idea.

Sunday . . . August 9

Cutting down hollyhocks today gave me a fore-taste of that nostalgia which fall brings to the gardener. Maybe the fact that I have been turning out Christmas copy this past week has advanced the seasons in my blood.

Monday . . . August 10

Visited an agricultural experiment station, in the interest of a fertilizer client, to see some test plots of new pasture grasses. Astonished to learn that we know less about grasses than about most other fodder crops. Asked the director how long it took, after a given agricultural practice was proved good, to get a majority of the farmers in his state to adopt it. He said about ten years. We spend millions on the most scientific production of knowledge, but do a horse-and-buggy job on the distribution of it in these fields where advertising is not relied upon.

Tuesday . . . August 11

In Washington, the City of Beautiful Nonsense. Found one place, at least, where they talk sense, namely, the Department of Commerce. Here they not only seem to have men who know what business is all about, but men who have kept their heads in all the hullabaloo which surrounds them. Elsewhere it must be the heat. It certainly is not the humility.

36

Wednesday . . . August 12

I would feel a lot happier about this war if I could get a conviction that anybody on our side had a plan for winning it. Maybe they have. If so, I know they can't tell me; and I know that I wouldn't be able to judge its merits if they did. But it doesn't take long to see a team on a field, or to see a new advertising campaign under way, to sense whether there is a plan behind it or merely improvisation.

Thursday . . . August 13

E. J. is one of our most brilliant copywriters, but he gets terrible fits of depression about his work. As with all really creative people, the frustrations of agency work get him down. Recommended to him today that he get himself a hobby which would be creative, but which called for tedious manual work. This is the best purgative for writer's crimps that I know.

Friday . . . August 14

All my working life I have been scaling photographs, art work, etc., for reduction, by the use of a diagonal line. This evening, scanning a popular book on mathematics, it suddenly burst on me that I had been using a well-known principle of geometry. My mathematical knowledge being practically nil, this discovery gave me the feeling that the stuff had some sense to it after all, and that maybe even I could learn it.

37

Saturday . . . August 15

A rainy day in the country—one of the pleasantest of life's interludes. Worked all day in the tool shop, with the rain drumming on the roof and the good smells of the wet earth coming in the open door. By supper time the creek was making music which could sing a man to sleep.

Sunday . . . August 16

Pleased to get from the editor some letters which indicate that, now and then, somebody reads this Diary. Showed them to my wife—who still wonders why. If a man likes the sound of words, putting them together may be its own reward. But I notice that a neighbor of mine, who often sits on his doorstep of an evening, playing a flute to himself, doesn't mind a little audience either.

Monday . . . August 17

Talked today with the domestic science editor of one of the women's magazines. She told me that she had tested literally thousands of recipes, covering almost every kind of food. Asked her what, after all this, she considered the best eating. She thought it was pretty hard to beat a good sirloin steak, washed down with straight whisky. Western gal.

Tuesday . . . August 18

Yesterday one of our clients was preparing to go

out of business at the end of this year. By then his stocks of WPB-controlled raw material would be exhausted. The amount that would be allowed him under rationing was too small for efficient operation; no substitute was in sight; nor had any way been found to convert his facilities to war production. Then suddenly, today, a supplier turned up with an offer to deliver enough material to keep him going well into next year. So now we are to rush a new campaign. If aspirin sales are booming here's the reason.

Wednesday . . . August 19

Do reading ratings, such as those furnished by Dr. Starch, measure only reading, or are they also reliable indicators of the sales effectiveness of ads? Interested today to find, in the case of two mail order pages of mine, that the variation in their direct sales figures was very closely paralleled by the variation in Dr. Starch's figures for the "read most" of the same pages. If we had enough cases like this we might answer this much debated question.

Thursday . . . August 20

Elmer Davis says that we are only ankle deep in this war, and that is right. But he implies that this is due to some failure on the part of the people, and that is wrong. The people are ready to dedicate themselves to total war, at whatever cost. The failure is in our leadership. They have moved in on parts of the economy, to control, direct, and support it. But they have left the rest to get along as best it can, and necessarily the men who operate this free economy must continue to fight their own battles rather than the nation's. When our leaders develop the vision, courage, and administrative skill to organize the nation for total war, the people will come along with them—and their consecration and power will shake the world.

Friday . . . August 21

Wrote a piece of copy today for a little two-page envelope stuffer which a client wanted. Maybe I shouldn't have "wasted" my time on it. But the merchandise was intriguing, I had an idea for it, and I just wanted to do it. I never could understand these copywriters who get excited only over a page in *Life*.

Saturday . . . August 22

Read with interest the dispatches from Washington about meat rationing. Wonder what they will do with a fellow like me, who has butchered his own steer and has 400 pounds of prime beef hanging in the ice house? Time to follow that domestic science woman's idea.

Sunday . . . August 23

See by the Exodus that the Lord had quite a time persuading Moses to take on the leadership of his people, and bring them out of Egypt. "And Moses said unto the Lord, Oh Lord, I am not eloquent:

40

for I am slow of speech, and of a slow tongue. And the Lord said unto him, Is there not Aaron thy brother? I know that he can speak well. He shall be thy spokesman unto the people: he shall be to thee a mouth, and thou shalt be to him instead of God." . . . The first advertiser-agency relationship.

Monday . . . August 24

Somebody in the office loaned Miss Malaprop her first copy of the *Reader's Digest.* I asked her how she liked it, and she looked slightly embarrassed. Said she didn't think the name was very refined— *Digest* sounded so physicological.

Tuesday . . . August 25

My favorite client came in today. Yes, I think it is true that every agent has one. He is not necessarily, or even usually, the one with the biggest appropriation; at least mine isn't. He is just the client for whom I work with the greatest satisfaction. He is tough, but fair. He makes me work hard, but he knows and appreciates good work when he sees it. He gives me his complete confidence, and makes me feel that his job, his ambitions, his problems, and his rewards are mine. So for him I go to the bottom of whatever I have.

Wednesday . . . August 26

Who says it is sometimes more important than what is said. C. E. Walberg, who had a big hand in government advertising in the last war, agrees with me that this is the point being overlooked now. He sends me a copy of a letter he has written Don Nelson begging him to have the government itself tell the people what it wants them to do. He cites chapter and verse on how it was done before. Here's hoping the big boy listens.

Thursday . . . August 27

Because words and phrases are regular Typhoid Marys of ideas, they have a power to inoculate us of which we are usually unconscious. When I was a boy we spoke of the retailer's occupation as "keeping store." That is, he *kept* the community's *store* of surplus goods until somebody needed them. And his whole business conduct was governed by this idea. By what words was he changed into the aggressive merchant, and when? Only thirty years ago, in 1912, I had a part in the preparation of the first book on "sales quotas." These were new words then, and they, with other phrases, projected a new concept of making every man do his duty as a consumer; making every community toe an advancing consumption mark. Held up to manufacturers' salesmen, who in turn held them up to retailers, they changed the whole face of business; indeed, of life itself. Whether for better or for worse affiant saith not.

Friday . . . August 28

We need to explore more than we have the appeal which different colors make to different people. I have begun to keep notes on the tastes displayed by my friends in their choice of such things as neckties, and I find that each man tends to follow one particular color range. This checks with my own responses: I am a sucker for browns and tans and have no use for the blues. What happens, then, when a product is packaged in only one color scheme?

Saturday . . . August 29

A free-running horse in a field is surely one of the most beautiful and invigorating sights in life. Watching my Palomino so disport himself, with mane and tail a-flying, I could not but feel more *élan* in myself.

Sunday . . . August 30

After a rainy night at the farm I was wakened by water dripping in my face. For the first time in my life I became roof conscious. My receptivity to roofing advertising has gone up at least a thousand per cent.

Monday . . . August 31

Musing on my leaky roof experience, and how it changed my interest in roofing advertising, I wondered if we consider this receptivity factor enough. We give plenty of thought to the seed we sow; perhaps not enough to the ground it falls on. Yet a friend in the medical business tells me that his test campaigns are often complicated by the differences

43

in morbidity, as he calls it, in two apparently similar towns. Another tells me that the consumption of chocolate products will vary, as between two given population units, depending on their racial make-up. We recognize the seasonal factor in receptivity, but how many other, less obvious ones do we overlook?

September, 1942

Tuesday . . . September 1

You can wrench fruit off a tree, or you can wait until it ripens and falls to your touch. I see lots of copy of the wrenching kind: it pulls too hard for a sale. Then I see copy which eases along, ripening the desire of the reader until the order falls. It takes hard writing to make easy reading, as Robert Louis Stevenson said. Even more, it takes hard thinking about the reader's wants to make one of those easygoing, fruitful advertisements.

Wednesday . . . September 2

All this trouble with India reminds me of the time I went there for one of the biggest American corporations. I found the British in that part of the world as cordial as game keepers on a private preserve. The publisher of *The Times of India*, the most important newspaper, couldn't understand what an American was doing out there, anyhow. The idea of paying an agency commission to one nearly gave him apoplexy. There was no room for American ideas. In such complete self-assurance the English have governed and developed the country magnificently on the physical side. Their difficulties come from the fact that they are completely unconscious of the psychological brutalities they commit in the process.

Thursday . . . September 3

A letter from an old copywriter friend tells me of the consummation of a dream. He has fixed it up with his boss to work six months in the agency business, and have the other six months off for his own pursuits—in the immediate future, war work. I know one writer who has been doing this with great success for years. Fields must lie fallow at times, and I note that all my fruit trees have their resting years. Perhaps all of our creative people would be more productive on some such basis.

Friday . . . September 4

William McFee winces when he sees "Ad Man" in my title. He thinks this shorter, more racy term is, as the English would say, cheap and nasty. I understand the feeling and sometimes share it. Ad Man does connote all the worst thoughts which the critics have about us, and if this Diary were not all in the family I might not use the term. But in the family I think it may have some virtues. Here I hope it connotes all the Diary pretends to be: just the plain account of a shirt sleeve worker, with a decent pride in his medium. More important, Ad Man sets its face against all those pompous pretensions which lead to such vulgarisms as realtor and mortician. Knowing the proneness of human beings to such delusions, Emerson said: Always call things by their lowest terms. There isn't any lower than Ad Man, so I guess I'll stick to that.

Saturday . . . September 5

Hauled 220 pounds of peaches into town and traded them to the grocer at 5c a pound. He will sell them for 7c, a very modest mark-up, considering the risk and spoilage he takes.

Sunday . . . September 6

Talked with a professor friend of mine who has developed an interesting technique for predicting what people will do, in mass. First, he locates the significant word symbols for certain ideas—say, social security, or free enterprise. Then he tabulates and charts the number of times these words appear in print, public speeches, etc., in (a) a negative or unfavorable use; (b) a positive or favorable use. If the chart shows a rising favorable use of the word the idea is making headway and the time when people will act upon it may be foreseen. Contrariwise, the idea is dying out. Could be applied, say in trade papers, to foresee changes in trade practices.

Monday . . . September 7

Several much appreciated letters have suggested

that these jottings should be made into a book. Maybe. But I have always felt that an ad man had better not have a book out against him until he was ready to retire. Then he might be able to begin one in some such fashion as Lord Bryce did his *American Commonwealth:* "Now that I am free from the reticences of a party man . . ."

Tuesday . . . September 8

Today my daughter began her advertising career —behind the counter of a grocery store. There, if she follows my advice, she will stay for six months, studying and recording how women buy food. She has a list of specific case studies to complete, such as, Do women ask for a can of milk or a can of Pet? What is their reaction to coffee in glass jars? And so on. In her spare time she will study stenography. Sundays off, of course.

Wednesday . . . September 9

Listening to a magazine representative today reminded me of my own two years as advertising manager of a small publication. It was then that I learned the representative's real handicap against the agent. His lack of equal knowledge of the advertiser's problems and policies always leaves him at a disadvantage. Representatives will recognize the similarity to the situation in a story told me by an Arab camel driver in Egypt. God, he said, has a Hundred Names. The Arab knows Ninety-Nine of them, but the Camel knows the Hundredth. And that, he said, is what gives the Camel his slightly supercilious look.

Thursday . . . September 10

The Lord knows that I am not a handsome man, nor one gifted with social graces. So in my youth the Apollos of this world often awed me. Tonight, out to dinner, I met one of them again. When I first met him, twenty years ago, he was already a high government official, and exuded success at every pore. I remember how he dazzled me. But since then I have learned that it pays to examine this type with particular attention to their mental horse power. This one proved to be just another Body by Fisher.

Friday . . . September 11

Recalling my note on Moses and Aaron, I thought on what a really good job Aaron did. There must be ten thousand who know Moses for one who remembers Aaron. A friend of mine who was raised in business by old J. Walter Thompson himself, says that one of that pioneer's constant admonitions was: Never let yourself get on the stage in front of your client. In this trade the "passion for anonymity" was well developed long before the White House ever heard of it.

Saturday . . . September 12

They say farming doesn't pay the city man, though I know one who has been collecting a neat 9% on his investment for several years. But the real pay-off is in education. In the city the contest is man against man. In the country it seems like man against all the rest of nature. You don't know nothing until you take that one on.

Sunday . . . September 13

Answered a timid knock at my door last night and found my old country-woman neighbor from up the road. She had a letter from her boy in the Army. He was okay; the Army was okay; don't worry, Ma; write me care the Postmaster, New York City. That was all she knew—and she wanted to know so much more. How many million mothers like her were scattered over the country that night? In how many were the same hopes and fears palpitating like heartbeats in the dark? Watch these mothers, Mr. Advertiser, Mr. Politician.

Monday . . . September 14

Sometimes under pressure, at white heat, you turn out the complete and perfect advertisement. At other times, with toil and trouble, rewrites and refinements, you finally get one to where it pleases you. In either case you send it off with some thrill of satisfaction and pride. Then a week, two weeks, a month later you see it, suddenly, in some publication. And you grimace and say, "My God. Did I do that?"

Tuesday . . . September 15

Had a visit from a young college man who has been aiming at advertising, but is now going into the Army. He asked: "Should I still be thinking of advertising, if and when I come back? Will there be any advertising then, or any opportunity in it?" Told him I thought this world now is in process of being made over—in its geography, its political and social organizations, its economics, and its technology. That the technological revolution alone—the new materials and productive processes—would mean a complete change in our living habits, as rapidly as man's mind could be brought abreast of this revolution. And that was a job advertising would have to do. The greatest, most exciting job in its history.

Wednesday . . . September 16

Talked with a Western newspaper publisher, who dropped in to make a courtesy call. I am always amazed anew at how remote many of these men seem to be from advertising, especially national advertising. Apparently they are kept so busy being leading citizens that they never have time to learn much about this bread and butter side of their business. One of them—and a very important one, too— once almost bragged to me that, while his paper had sold millions of dollars' worth of space, he hadn't the faintest idea how advertising paid anybody.

Thursday . . . September 17

A letter today from an old friend who left the advertising business some years ago and went into educational work. Now he wishes he hadn't. It reminded me of that essay by the witty Dr. Crowther, "On Every Man's Desire to Be Somebody Else." If you want to reach a man's real ego, he said, tell a preacher what a great lawyer he would have made; a lawyer what a great industrialist or statesman. When we ad men get these yearnings to be somebody else we are only suffering from a very common complaint. I have lived through several severe attacks of it myself. Now I suspect that I will never develop half the capacities that this job really calls for.

Friday . . . September 18

Looking through the current *American Magazine*, after hours, I was set to pondering by the Four Roses color page there. It made me think how far-reaching the ad man's influence may sometimes be on the manners and customs of his time. For I venture the belief that this advertisement will not only sell the product, but that its illustration by Falter will also (1) promote drinking like a gentleman; (2) do something to make urbanity in men a model; (3)

52

have an effect on styles in men's dress; and (4) incidentally, influence illustrative techniques. So thinking, finished my Old Fashioned, and caught my train.

Saturday . . . September 19

There is an old well and well-house in our farmyard, and the old oaken bucket still hangs there. Nowadays we pump water from it and carry it under pressure to the house. When the pump goes wrong, and I have to carry water and heat it for a shave, I ain't fit to live with. But when I come in from the orchard after a morning's work, a drink still tastes sweeter when hauled up by hand.

Sunday . . . September 20

Seeing here reference to my visit to an agricultural experiment station, the secretary of the *Journal of Agricultural Engineering* was good enough to send me an article on the drying of fodder crops. Today I got around to reading it, and couldn't wait till I got my farmer to do the same. I have been telling him for a long time that there ought to be some way to dry alfalfa and put it right into the bale, without taking the risk from rain during cutting. But he thought that was just another of my fool notions. He still thinks so.

Monday . . . September 21

An A.P. dispatch today reports Don Nelson as again making a speech portraying the horrors to come in our civilian life. All right, Don, we can take them, when and as they come. What we wish you fellows in Washington would do is keep your energies for frightening Japs.

Tuesday . . . September 22

The death of Condé Nast reminds me of one of his penetrating sayings which I always greatly believed in. A publisher, he said, is only a name broker. His job is to devise an editorial appeal which will bring together a list of a certain kind of names, access to which he can then sell to advertisers. Perhaps only an ad man who has had experience testing different lists of names with direct mail can fully appreciate the point of this. But I always thought that if more publishers defined their job as sharply, and more publications were chosen on the list of names basis, advertising would be more productive.

Wednesday . . . September 23

The heart of every advertisement, of course, is the proposition it makes the reader: do this and get that. Theoretically, it is the manufacturer's job to devise this proposition in the designing of his product. But products tend to remain static, while markets tend to be highly dynamic. So more often than not the ad man finds himself forced to develop a new proposition into which the product can be

54

fitted, or to which it can be reshaped. In doing so he becomes, in fact, the interpreter of the public to the manufacturer, the true consumer representative.

Thursday . . . September 24

Spent this morning with one of my mail order clients, shucking the incoming mail. There is no fun like it. From the customers' letters I get a feel for the proposition which nothing else will give me. And from the handling of checks, money orders, and currency I get the only balm there is for the copywriters' itch for orders.

Friday . . . September 25

How much of the actor must there be in the copywriter? In the mail I handled yesterday there was a letter from a prominent citizen of New York, addressed to the fictitious character I had created for this client. It said: "In sending you the enclosed order, I want to compliment you on your advertisement. It was honest, it was frank, it was refreshing. You made monkeys out of all the self-instituted master copywriters." When the villain is hissed may he not claim a convincing performance?

Saturday . . . September 26

Talked with a chain store fruit buyer, to see if he would handle some of my apple crop. Got an order from him for early delivery, at a fair price.

The chains have very smartly learned that the local producer is a good friend to have.

Sunday . . . September 27

Called from my Sunday reflections by a long distance query whether I would take a job with one of the Washington war agencies. Find myself sorely perplexed how to answer. We all know that our lives themselves are on call. But this particular agency is in a mess. Its organization is bad. It has already broken the reputations and spirits of many men, and will break more. I would rather fight this war on any front than the Washington one. I must sleep on it.

Monday . . . September 28

The question as to my taking a job in Washington decided for me, thank the Lord, by my sponsor's discovery that I am *persona non grata* to certain influential New Dealers. It is said that I have slept too often in the bed of Big Business.

Tuesday . . . September 29

Studying the records of an "on approval" offer today, I uncovered the hard fact that ministers of the gospel are among the poorest risks. They seem to take too literally that line about the forgiveness of debts.

56

Wednesday . . . September 30

A Washington newspaper tried to do away with its society column; *Time* says the day of the social-ite (a term it invented) is over; *The New Yorker* seems to agree; and a popular motion picture is built around the resentment of ordinary English-men to their upper crust. These are signs of the times which might seem to indicate a passing of the snob appeal, of society women testimonials, and such. But I have my doubts whether it is more than a spell of cloudy weather. Every society which the anthropologists have ever studied has had its *elite*, whose doings were a matter of great curiosity to the rest. Even in Russia today the engineers seem to be developing into such a class.

October, 1942

Thursday . . . October 1

Talked with a competitor who has built a fine reputation as an interpreter of the public service side of business. But he was bemoaning his inability to get and hold package goods accounts. Tried to console him with the classic example of a great reputation in one field proving a handicap in another, namely, when Mark Twain had to publish his cherished life of Joan D'Arc under another pen name, in order to have it taken seriously.

Friday . . . October 2

Presented a new campaign to a client today and he didn't like it. He couldn't tell me why, but instead began trying to tell me how to make the ads over. This is one route to poor advertising. A manufacturer usually has an inarticulate "feel" for his business which will tell him when an ad is wrong. In such cases the agent's job is to bore in and find the roots of that feeling. Once he has, he is quite likely to know best how to make the ads right.

58

Saturday . . . October 3

Spent the morning nailing shooks into apple boxes, out in the dappled sunlight and shadows of the orchard. As pleasant work as a man could have, with the pungent resin smell of the boxes in his nostrils, and the fine October sky overhead.

Sunday . . . October 4

Pondering further on the place of the *elite*, it occurred to me that in all this talk about "freedoms," the one that nobody promises is the freedom to complete social equality with your neighbor. Both Democracy and Christianity originally implied that promise, but neither was able to fulfill it. Economic equality, political equality, and even equality in the sight of God are as nothing when they come up against that intangible but powerful thing called social status—as every woman knows.

Monday . . . October 5

Washington officials continue to bare their teeth at the Little Red Riding Hood of business. Today I counted three dire predictions in the morning headlines, and read several more in a Washington news-letter. Sure, things are going to get tougher and tougher; but we could meet the real problems with steadier nerves if there weren't so many big, bad wolves making faces in the dark.

Tuesday . . . October 6

Today I was getting out a piece of fine printed matter—a reproduction of a rare object of art, intended to be preserved as such. I had helping me a first rate art director and upper case typographer. It might be supposed that with such talent and experience as the three of us possessed we could have gone direct to the creative mark, and produced the final and perfect form at first trial. But it took a dozen dummies before we were satisfied to let one go to the printer. Inspiration and flair are great qualities in this business, but for real results give me the man who never quits trying.

Wednesday . . . October 7

Visiting this evening in the home of a couple with young children, I heard the wife say: "Sunday is such a long day; let's plan now something to do on this coming one." A very significant remark, I thought, and an expression of what millions feel among our urban families. With the Sunday automobile ride passing out, what have you to offer against the tedium of the American Sunday, Mr. Advertiser? Perhaps this is the chance for our churches to modernize their appeal and stage a come-back.

Thursday . . . October 8

It is interesting to observe the differing effects of the war on the human spirit. I find some clients who are already spiritually licked by the mounting difficulties they face. But today I listened to one present to his board of directors a plan for a new and farseeing development of their business—one which required a large investment now for post war fruition. Its reception demonstrated again the magic truth in Daniel Burnham's phrase: Make no little plans.

Friday . . . October 9

The degree to which advertising is now understood and accepted as an essential tool of business would amaze a practitioner of twenty years ago. Today I talked with a client who literally has no selling problem; all he has to do is to allocate to his distributors that part of his production which the Army has not taken. Yet he told me that his directors, including a banker, had approved a recommendation of mine for the doubling of their appropriation. Prelude to a pleasant week-end!

Saturday . . . October 10

Gave my annual cider-making party at the farm. Long ago learned that week-end guests are happiest when kept at work. An old-fashioned, hand cider press and bushels of apple culls are ideal for the purpose. Each guest departs with his own gallon jugful, pleased as Punch with himself. And I contemplate the barrel in my cellar with equal satisfaction.

Sunday . . . October 11

Dipped into one of the Unity of Science series being issued by the University of Chicago. Most of it beyond me—which convinced me again that science needs englishing by ad men. But one section on the part which controlled experiments have played in the development of the physical sciences proved extremely interesting. We will never bring a real science of advertising into being until we find better ways to use this experimental technique.

Monday . . . October 12

Lunched today with a client of many years standing, who got to reminiscing about this and that. Among other things, we reviewed with satisfaction the great development of a new product which I had first suggested to him several years ago. With a perfectly straight face, and complete sincerity, he said: "Yes, it has been a great success. I have often wondered how I ever came to have such a good idea."

Tuesday . . . October 13

Went into the New York office of another agent with whom I am cooperating on a war campaign, and noted on his wall the reproduction of a portrait of William H. Johns. This is the second one of these I have seen in agency offices other than BBD&O. I know of no other agent who is so honored by his competitors. Years ago, when Bill Johns was the head of the George Batten Company, I became a very small client of that agency. Going out to lunch one day with the account executive, we met Mr. Johns in the elevator, and I was introduced to him as a new client. With some heat he turned on the account man and said: "Then why haven't I met Mr. Young before?" This made such an impression on a young and obscure advertising manager that he never forgot it, and never had any difficulty understanding why such a man had both the respect and affection of his trade.

Wednesday . . . October 14

Spent the day in Washington, taking advantage of a fortunate opportunity to talk off the record with some of the managers of our war machine. There seems to be no doubt that we are making real progress; but equally there is no doubt that we could have made a great deal more. From all I can learn I cannot escape the conclusion that most of our failures stem directly from the congenital unwillingness of the President to delegate power and authority along with responsibility. But no one whose voice has carrying power seems willing to say this—and that is disturbing. It smacks too much of the *King can do no wrong*.

Thursday . . . October 15

Started out on a day train through Virginia, in order to see what war-time travel conditions really are. Found the whole countryside awash and every stream at flood from three days' heavy rain. All day we inched along, past stations with famous Civil War names, and across rivers carrying tons of priceless top soil to the sea. We tend to think of erosion as largely a western problem, but this northern Virginia country shows some of the worst I have seen.

Friday . . . October 16

Our train twenty-five hours late, so I have plenty of time to observe the travelers and travel conditions. We carry fifteen cars, mostly day coaches, heavily weighted with soldiers and sailors on individual jaunts. Two types stand out: youths of the automobile age, who have practically never been on a train before; and people of all ages who have never traveled in Pullmans before, and are obviously unfamiliar with their amenities.

Saturday . . . October 17

I hated to do it, but today I had to kill a striking new campaign, worked out in my absence by one of our writers and art directors. The layouts were fresh and interesting, and the text smoothly written. But the ideas were feeble, and no amount of beautiful expression could make them otherwise. The old, old error of relying on form instead of substance.

Sunday . . . October 18

Picked up Miriam Beard's "History of the Business Man" and tried for the third or fourth time to read it. Finally decided that my impatience with it was due to a certain glibness with which the author drew deductions from second- or third-hand material. This set up a desire for some first-hand reporting, so looked for my copy of Plutarch's "Lives," but could not find it, and picked up Boswell's "Life of Johnson" instead. Read this with much contentment all evening, finding many a bit in it useful to the copywriter who would study how to use words to bring a subject to life.

Monday . . . October 19

If a man sits down, as I did this evening, to list his objectives—to get clearly before him what it is he is trying to do with his life over the next few years—he must inevitably put at the top of the list: Help win the war. Until he has polarized his thinking with regard to this supreme objective he cannot function effectively anywhere. But too many men in advertising, who clearly see or feel this, are jumping too quickly to the conclusion that this means abandoning their work for something more directly labeled war. Advertising, too, can serve in total war, and skill in its use is not lightly to be thrown overboard in any sensible allocation of manpower.

Tuesday . . . October 20

An incident in our office today made me conscious again of the wide gap that often exists between employer and employe psychology. I am not a Christian Scientist, but on this I would go with them: that as a man thinketh so is he. To begin your rise out of the employe class, begin to think as an employer.

Wednesday . . . October 21

A letter from a client, commenting on a successful advertisement, says his only objection is that the copy is too long. I verily believe that if a good advertisement were shown to a newborn babe in his crib this would be his first comment on it. In short, the fear of long copy seems to be congenital —and persistent. This in spite of the facts (a) that people buy publications solely for the purpose of reading; and (b) that every direct mail advertiser has proved over and over again that the more you tell the quicker you sell.

Thursday . . . October 22

Looking over a current weekly I get the feeling that we are still producing too many pages which do nothing but boast of Zilch's contribution to the war. This is dangerous to the whole advertising structure. Every one of these pages ought to be put to work speeding the public's adjustments to war-time living. On that course advertising is unassailable.

Friday . . . October 23

Lunching with a sales manager, it was brought home to me how the shortage in many kinds of consumers' goods is now bringing about a sort of unconscious acceptance of the principles of selective selling, which many companies formerly resisted. The desirable but hard-to-sell dealers, whom their salesmen always tended to dodge, are now crying for goods; and many a line is getting placement in stores which it had coveted for years. The smart boys will see this as an opportunity which they may never have again, and will adjust their distribution program accordingly.

Saturday . . . October 24

Grey and cold at the farm, with snow signals flying in the sky. But the frost is on the pumpkin and the fodder in the barn. The apples are all picked, packed, and stored. The hogs seem determined to overcome the drop in prices. And the elected turkey is fattening in his pen. In short, every sight begins to spell that most spontaneous of all the holy days, Thanksgiving.

Sunday . . . October 25

Every artist knows that sunlight can only be pictured with shadows. And every good biographer shows us, as Boswell did, that only the faults of a great man make him real to us. But in advertising we are afraid of this principle, hence less convincing than we might be. The most extraordinary response I ever got to an ad was when I offered a second-hand motor car for sale, and judiciously described its defects as well as its virtues.

Monday . . . October 26

In this time of profound emotional tension it is natural that there should be a reaching for lofty themes in advertising. But I wonder whether we may not be overdoing it. I observe (1) that at the very time when cloth needs saving, women all the way from *Vogue* to Montgomery Ward develop a cape style of wearing coats which flaunts the uselessness of sleeves; (2) that even the boys on the bombing fronts still want to know the sports scores; and (3) that most of my middle-aged friends are still worrying about their waistlines. So maybe the homely things are still worth dealing with. As the beer people say, morale is a lot of little things.

Tuesday . . . October 27

Lunching with a publisher, we talked about the rise and fall of different magazines over the last quarter of a century. Perhaps nothing else illustrates so well the economic maxim that "wealth is a flow and not a fund." Successful publishing properties are built by men with dynamic instincts for the flow of things. Their decline begins when they fall into the hands of corporations controlled by counting house brains, whose instincts are for preserving the funds. This stops the flow, and the wealth seeps away, no man knows how.

Wednesday . . . October 28

Telephoned by a mighty hunter to come and eat some pheasants which he had brought home from North Dakota; but had to take a train out of town instead. I never cease to be astounded at the relatively high percentage of his income this man will spend on his hunting trips and equipment. The worst nickel pinchers I know are the same when it comes to any hobby. If I wanted a business that would withstand the fall of empires I think I would pick one in the hobby field.

Thursday . . . October 29

Made a presentation to a prospective advertiser who wants to start a new brand in an already well supplied field. But it is a field which is slowly expanding through natural causes, and it is probable that another brand can find a place in it. Especially if, as I suspect is true in this case, the cost of entry is reduced by the present tax situation.

Friday . . . October 30

Now comes the open season for the great American sport of speech making. Invitations to make speeches and to listen to speeches pour in. Personally I like to hear myself talk. I like that first moment when I wait for the audience to coalesce and come to me. And I like that last moment, when they are held in suspense on a high note, and then dismissed to the relief of applause. It is only the birth pangs which I know I will have in preparing a talk which keep me from indulging this taste for histrionics.

Saturday . . . October 31

Returning from the movies this afternoon I thought how like they are in some ways to advertising. The exaggerations which people complain of in both are not so much due to an intent to deceive, as they are to a lack of skill in striking the true note. Camera men and ad men alike live too much on the surface of their callings, and lean too heavily on the tricks of their trade. Only as they send their roots down into the subsoil of life itself do they learn not to do violence to its integrity.

November, 1942

Sunday . . . November 1

Read with interest that piece in the *Reader's Digest* about long range weather forecasting. I have noted here before the importance of factors affecting receptivity to our messages, and weather is probably one of the important ones. We all recognize this when a dealer puts up a window sticker for raincoats on a rainy day; or when Aunt Jemima says "I'se in town, honey!" on a frosty morning. But I suspect that if careful records were kept of variations in weather and advertising response, they would be found to correlate on a good many more products than we think.

Monday . . . November 2

Harried all day by problems arising from the suddenly imposed salary limitation orders. Two important radio contracts about to be signed are completely up in the air because no lawyer seems to know how to interpret the orders in application to them. An art director with a tempting offer from another agency wonders whether he can ever earn as much here, and I can't tell him. Rumors reach me of similar unsettlements among other staff people. The Lord knows I am in no mood to vote tomorrow for a continuance of such administrative ineptitude.

Tuesday . . . November 3

Lunched with a friend whose firm, greatly expanded with war work, now has forty thousand employes. The appalling problem they will face in keeping these people employed in the post-war period now begins to worry them. The fact that such firms are showing a sense of social responsibility for this problem is one of the most hopeful signs I see. Advertising men who wonder what contribution they are making to the war effort itself might well look to this collateral problem for their answer.

Wednesday . . . November 4

The defeat of Senator Norris reminds me of a day I lunched with him in the Senate restaurant, and heard him say: "All I hope for is to serve long enough to see the money taken away from the men who have too much, and distributed to my people." This sincere old man, too, failed to grasp that wealth is a flow, and not a fund. Like so many New Dealers he wanted to treat it as a fixed sum to be divided up. In the attempts to do so he discouraged the flow and all the spreading blessings thereof.

72

Thursday . . . November 5

Watching an advertiser sit on the edge of his chair as the results of a market survey were presented to him, I realized how eternal springs the hope that this kind of mechanism will furnish all the answers. But it never does. Useful as such work is in telling us what people are doing, there still remains the problems of why they do it, and how to disturb their doings. Only creative imaginations can find the answers.

Friday . . . November 6

When my friend Langdon Mitchell, the playwright, was a young man he took one of his plays to Mrs. Fiske, the leading actress of her day. Having sweated over its writing for a year or more he was appalled to have her say: "Now, Mr. Mitchell, this is all right except the third act. Run around the corner to the saloon and fix that up, and come back in a couple of hours." Having to do it, he did; and the play was a great success. Writers who demand the perfect surroundings are kidding themselves. I have always been glad myself that, in my first copywriting job, I had to work in a large open room, with all the confusion of a general office around me.

Saturday . . . November 7

Brought in a box of my Golden Delicious apples from the farm and sampled them among various friends. The first crisp bite, and the juice running down the lips, sells them. The real contribution we city fellows can make to farming is in insisting on high production standards, practices, and controls to produce a quality product. I find few farmers who have the rigid manufacturing viewpoint of my best clients.

Sunday . . . November 8

At last, from North Africa, comes news which indicates that we have a real plan for winning this war. This gives me more cheer than even the Egyptian victory. As one of our greatest advertisers used to say: "A weak policy strongly pursued is better than no policy at all, or than a strong policy weakly pursued."

Monday . . . November 9

Today I spent more than two hours trying to keep an effective campaign from being spoiled. Everybody agreed that it had been wonderful as it had been running. Nobody would think of changing its basic plan or appeal. But couldn't this part just be expanded a little; couldn't this new element be added? And so on, in a dozen different ways. Oh these foxes, these little foxes that eat away the vines!

Tuesday . . . November 10

Talked with an English advertising man, whom I had met in London, who has been sent here, not to make propaganda, but to explore the causes of mis-understandings between us. Nothing is more important now and for the post-war period than friendship and mutual respect among the English-speaking peoples. I should be sorry to be thought lacking in such feelings, as one of my Canadian readers recently thought I was. As it happens, I am a great admirer of English life and people; but I do think they have some mannerisms, attitudes, and customs which are not calculated to win friends and influence people, and about which their best friends might tell them. Anyhow, that is what this man said he wanted to know, so I took him at his word.

Wednesday . . . November 11

Learned today that we have lost from our ranks my old friend "Dinkie" Dallis, best known and best loved advertising man of the deep South. He started, as did so many of our older generation, as a newspaper man. As a cub reporter on the old *Atlanta Constitution* he scooped the world on the assassination of President McKinley. He always knew a story when he saw one, and could always tell one with the art of the born *raconteur*. Be sure to tell St. Peter that one about the female Holy Roller, Dinkie.

Thursday . . . November 12

At breakfast in a crowded diner, coming into Chicago from New York, there sat down opposite me a boyish fellow in a well-worn uniform. On his breast was the insignia of the Royal Air Force, but on his left shoulder was U.S.A. For over a year he had been one of the Spitfire fighters, but all he would talk about was how the London blackout got on his nerves. Now he was transferring to our naval aviation, and had ten days' leave to see his folks in Colorado. So we parted. But just for this moment I brushed the wing of one of that gallant few to whom so many of us, as well as the English, owe so much.

Friday . . . November 13

Received a copy of the Mead bill, recently introduced in the Senate, which advertising men might well study. This bill declares it to be the policy of the United States to *maintain* small independent businesses of the country, and directs the Secretary of Commerce to set up personnel to conduct research for, and counsel with, small business owners on such problems as location, manufacturing processes, distribution, domestic and foreign markets, merchandising, accounting, etc., etc. All at an estimated cost of $10,000,000 to begin with. Such a proposal raises many questions. For example: Do we want to *maintain* small business in the distribution field even if larger ones prove they can lower the cost of marketing?

Saturday . . . November 14

A fine frosty morning and a clear sky overhead, so took my gun and my old dog Butch to beat the hedge rows and coverts in my and the neighbors' fields. I am not much of a shot, and do not have that zest for the kill which makes a mighty hunter. But we came home with enough for the pot to gladden the heart of the meat rationer, and with the best of appetites to enjoy it.

Sunday . . . November 15

Started reading Peter Drucker's "Future of Industrial Man," having gotten so much out of his earlier book on "The End of Economic Man." The future of advertising depends so much on how we solve the problems these books discuss, and Drucker is such a refreshing thinker about them, that I consider him required reading. In fact, I am grateful to Hitler for driving this young Austrian over here.

Monday . . . November 16

The North African affair brings ancient Carthage back into the news, and the Roman Senator who kept hammering home: "Carthage must be destroyed." If I remember correctly, it took him some twenty years of such repetition to get results. In contrast, when Hannibal, the Carthaginian general, wanted to get his army across the supposedly impassable Alps to attack Rome, he said to his troops, in effect: "Boys, across the Alps lies Italy, with its fertile fields and sunny plains. There is wine, and women and loot. Let's go!" And they went, right

77

then . . . Such is the difference between a slogan and a good piece of selling copy.

Tuesday . . . November 17

One of the signs of the improved position of advertising with business managements is the improvement in the caliber of advertising managers and directors. It used to be that the good men who developed in this field were rather quickly drawn off into agencies. But that does not appear to be so true today. We now have numerous companies which have placed their advertising directors up among the top management group, with a resulting increase in dignities and rewards which proves attractive to first rate men.

Wednesday . . . November 18

Scanning some expense accounts today I noticed, as I long have, that the cost of entertaining clients does not vary so much by clients as it does by agency representatives. Some representatives just have a natural taste for night life which clients furnish an excuse for cultivating. And I have observed over the years that the less sure a man is of having something within himself to deliver, the more he depends on the Great White Way. In fact, excessive entertainment accounts are now to me a symptom of a man so weak he should be gotten rid of.

Thursday . . . November 19

Today I was solicited to take an active part in the state affairs of the revived Republican party. But both by temperament and conviction I am and always will be a mugwump in politics. I hold that the constant effort of the advertising man should be to train his mind to complete objectivity in the scrutiny of social trends and forces of every kind. It is hard enough to do this at the best, without adding the handicap of political partisanship.

Friday . . . November 20

A well-known agency man, who has been very successful, told me today that he had tried to write down what reasons there were, besides vanity and greed, why he should not retire. He could think of none. As he thinks further, of course, he will find the real reason is the desire to use the powers which he has developed within himself; to do his stuff, as we say. This is a psychological urge from which he will never escape.

Saturday . . . November 21

Gradually the situation with regard to the government use of advertising seems to be clarifying itself, thanks to the joint efforts of OWI and the Advertising Council. There are big jobs to be done; and for the present, at least, industry will have to do them, insofar as financing is concerned. But the actual work load will fall mostly on the agencies, and no agency man who isn't drafted will need to go looking for war work elsewhere.

Sunday . . . November 22

Visited with an advertising man who has worked for years in a Latin American country. He told me that it was easy in most cases to adapt a successful campaign here to use there. Differences in language, mechanics, and customs have to be taken care of, but the basic idea and appeal can often be the same. This checks with my own observations abroad. In every country I have seen, women want to be beautiful and men want to make money; and advertising often speaks the true universal language.

Monday . . . November 23

There is an intangible but very important element in any good piece of copy which too seldom gets the consideration it deserves. This is the impact of the personality of the writer upon the reader. Radio, more than any other medium, demonstrates quite clearly how powerful a sales force this personality-plus may be. In printed copy it must be transmitted largely through the writer's choice of words, and through his rhythm. Few advertisers seem to understand this, and do not know how often they edit this valuable ingredient out of copy.

80

Tuesday . . . November 24

There is one group in this business which is deeply disturbed by the income-limitation philosophy. It is made up of those who, with ten to fifteen years' apprenticeship behind them, have just reached the place where the next ten years might bring them economic security. Now they wonder whether that chance is gone for their lifetime, and what the substitutes for that hope are.

Wednesday . . . November 25

En route this evening to the old homestead in Ohio, for the Thanksgiving week-end. The train literally sold out, with customers standing in the aisles of all the coaches. Apparently many felt as I did— that this might be the last chance for a family get-together for some time to come.

Thursday . . . November 26

Sighted turkey. Sank same.

Friday . . . November 27

In Cincinnati found the first day of Christmas shopping going full blast. The merchants had given the downtown streets a festive air, and the public had responded. Traffic seemed to be on a pre-rationing spree; sidewalks were crowded; stores packed; and the hotels full of pretty girls and uniforms. At a newsstand I heard a woman ask: "Have you any magazines that are not full of war stories?"

Saturday . . . November 28

Took the Morgan mare for a morning ride along the river road. She is not as young as she used to be, but her spirit is as willing and her disposition as sweet as ever—qualities which, in the long haul, add up to more than youth and beauty, in either a horse or a woman.

Sunday . . . November 29

I believe that one of the deep-running currents of our time is a sort of emotional revolt against the machine age. While individually we want the conveniences it has brought us, there are millions who have a sort of terror at what the assembly line has done to their lives. Hence a nostalgia for the things that symbolize a simpler day, such as farms, hand craftsmanship, and Early American designs. When an advertiser taps such an underground current he gets a sure flow of business; and I wonder why more have not divined the existence of this one.

Monday . . . November 30

Spent some time this evening studying report No. 53 in the Continuing Study of Newspaper Reading. In the paper checked there were twelve small reader-type medical ads, and each of these got a reader rating of only 1% of the men and 1% of the women. Yet it is probable that every one of these ads is a tested seller of merchandise, without the aid of any other selling force. One of them, which I happen to know about, has been running without change for more than three years, and has made a marked increase in the sales of its product. The deduction would seem to be that such ads get a reading only from that small group with the specific ailments featured; but that they sell so effectively among this group as to pay a profit.

December, 1942

Tuesday . . . December 1

An advertiser, not a client, asked today for the name of the man who had written a particular series of ads which he admired. It was impossible to tell him, because the series as a whole was a group product. While one man conceived the basic idea, three others wrote individual pieces in the series; a research assistant dug up material for them; an art director dramatized the presentation; and a type man styled it. In this process the whole group cross-fertilized one another, and the resulting product is undoubtedly better than any one of the group alone could have produced.

Wednesday . . . December 2

Lunched today with a man whom I first knew, a good many years ago, as an agency copywriter. Now he is the head of a big and successful manufacturing company, marketing many advertised products. Sometimes advertising men are accused of being incapable of understanding any other than the promotional side of business. But this man, without losing his very keen instinct for the public's reactions,

84

has become a broad gauged executive, with a pro-
nounced flair for the management of men, materials,
and money.

Thursday . . . December 3

A friend from Washington dropped in, and we
fell to discussing the senatorial ambitions of a politician whom we both knew. I suggested that he had
the first requisite for a successful senator, namely,
the complete lack of a sense of humor. My friend
thought this a little rough on senators, but when I
asked him to name three with a sense of humor he,
who knows them all, proved unable to do so.

Friday . . . December 4

Busy all day with voluntary advertising work for
one of the government agencies. Unfortunately, it
has to pass through the hands of a former newspaper man, who is their public relations director.
Our top government officials do not understand that
most such men not only do not know anything
about the techniques of advertising, but are often
prejudiced against its use. This is the hardest hurdle
advertising has to get over in making a contribution
to the war effort.

Saturday . . . December 5

A correspondent takes me to task for an awkward
construction in a sentence recently published here.

85

I am afraid he is correct. I learned to write by ear, and have never been too sure of the rules of syntax and grammar. Even when I do know them, I often violate them—if I think that color, force, or rhythm can be gained by doing so. The English define a gentleman as one who is never unconsciously insulting. I try to maintain the same point of view toward the textbooks on language; but, through ignorance and carelessness, do not always succeed.

Sunday . . . December 6

Holed up in a hotel room all day, pounding away on my faithful Corona. Not my idea of the way to spend a bright Sunday, but it had to be done if several jobs were to make their deadlines. Now this final entry; and so to bed, as a famous diarist said. But with that purged feeling which comes from a clean job slate.

Monday . . . December 7

Coming along the street with an old-time newspaper representative, a passing Sandwich Man reminded him of a story. In the early days, he said, J. Walter Thompson was coming home one evening on the Third Avenue El, from his office in lower New York. Next to him was an old codger who opened a conversation, in the course of which he asked Mr. Thompson what business he was in. When he heard that it was advertising he said, with delight: "Why, so am I!" Then he added, reflec-

86

tively: "Ain't it hell when the wind blows?" . . . A point with which many an agent could have agreed during the past year.

Tuesday . . . December 8

One of the stars on our service flag now represents a boy who is "missing in action." And two of my close friends have now lost sons in the South Pacific. Quite suddenly the machine guns are chattering where I can hear them.

Wednesday . . . December 9

The late E. T. Gundlach broke many a lance against the general advertiser's indifference to the lessons of mail order advertising. It is true that the problems are not identical, and that the limitations and rigidities of mail order selling would sometimes defeat the larger purposes of another type of business. But in one respect, at least, it would seem that every type of advertiser has the same problem; namely, to be believed. The mail order man knows nothing so potent for this purpose as the testimonial, yet the general advertiser seldom uses it.

Thursday . . . December 10

Today I wanted to page Diogenes and show him an honest man. It came about in a meeting of a war work committee, where an agent and one of his clients found themselves on opposite sides of a difficult question. Many an agent would have straddled or held his peace, but this one laid it on the line. Afterward another member of the committee spoke of the agent's courage, but it seemed to me to be his honesty—the relation of which to courage is closer than is sometimes recognized.

Friday . . . December 11

Talked with the head of a great corporation, whose business volume is in the hundreds of millions. He told me that advertising costs were now the largest single item in their business—exceeding the costs of labor, materials, plant depreciation, or other selling. To such a man advertising has ceased to be something which somebody sells him, and has become a major business facility. He is as concerned with maintaining the freedom to use it as any medium owner or advertising agent could be.

Saturday . . . December 12

A growing pleasure which comes to me from these jottings is the correspondence, critical or otherwise, from readers. Today comes an entertaining letter from Garrick Taylor of Chicago, throwing up his hands in mock horror at my reference to Carthage and Rome. He fears that Thurman Arnold may some day use against us the fact that Hannibal's selling copy eventually brought him to disaster, while Cato's slogan became a reality. What I was trying to illustrate, of course, is the difference in

88

speed of two different persuasive techniques. From the technician's standpoint, in advertising as in medicine, many an operation has points of interest even though the patient dies from causes beyond the operator's control.

Sunday . . . December 13

Heard indirectly from an ad man in Washington, engaged in psychological warfare. When asked to describe his job he said it was "to drive the Nazis nuts." A job definition recommended to the Civil Service Commission as a model.

Monday . . . December 14

Read over the typed copy of an ad which I had written last night, and knew it was wrong. Went over it again and again before I was willing to see that I had fallen into one of the oldest traps of the copywriter's mind. Smack in the middle of the copy I had attempted to expound a pet idea of my own, which had only a tenuous connection with the theme. Once I faced up to that fact, and ruthlessly weeded out my pet, the copy flowed smoothly to its ordained end.

Tuesday . . . December 15

Lunching in a fashionable New York restaurant I was reminded again how much we need a social atlas of the United States. Markets are formed not

89

so much by geography, age, sex, or income as they are by social groupings of every kind. It is the standards set by the different groups to which we belong—trade, lodge, church, neighborhood, etc.—which really set most of our habits. Discussing this one day with a noted anthropologist, who held that the group was the key to every individual's life, he said it would take at least two years of hard work just to make a list of all such groups in a country as complex as this one.

Wednesday . . . December 16

The year's billing figures are now about complete. They show, by the grace of God, that we have had the biggest year in our history, with the largest net profit before taxes. So draws to a close a year that began with many dire prophecies of gloom, and again most of the things we have feared have not come upon us.

Thursday . . . December 17

Two years ago I suggested to an advertiser that he hire an economist as a permanent member of his staff. He was mildly interested in the thought, but did nothing about it. Today he asked me to find him such a man. More and more the rugged individualists are coming to see that there are forces beyond their control and ken; that these forces make up the social climate in which they have to work; that it is essential to try to foresee the direction in which these forces are traveling; and that alone they are ill-equipped to do so.

Friday . . . December 18

It seems likely to me that next year the biggest single classification of advertising will be that which is selling ideas instead of goods. Included in this will be industry-financed advertising for government. Both our publication pages and the radio disclose the growing pains which our writers are having in adapting to this fact. Some of them are going pretty far afield for their subject matter, and are slopping over with their "fine" writing of it. I still think the best bet, and the patriotic one, is to find for each advertiser the logical home front field to which he can make an informative contribution.

Saturday . . . December 19

Hauled a truck load of hogs to market and collected an average of $27.15 per head. Having started them as weaners at an average cost of $4.35, I came tooling home at sundown, composing in my head a poem on farming as a way of life.

Sunday . . . December 20

Leon Henderson's going may pacify Congress, but it will not change the fact that rationing is going to make government a burr under every citizen's saddle. It is interesting to speculate on what this will do to political trends. My guess is that it will help reverse the tendency of the past ten years to look to an all-wise, all-powerful government for the solution of all our problems. Also that the business man may regain some lustre by contrast.

Monday . . . December 21

Talked with a man recently from India. He said that we are publishing there newspaper advertisements explaining America's war aims. When I asked who signed them he said, The United States of America. When I asked who paid for them he said, The Office of War Information. This is advertising as it should be used by government. Why can it be so used in India and not here? Presumably for the sole reason that there are no publishers in India who can bleat to Congressmen when they are left off the list. Perhaps if all our publishers would sign a pledge not to use such pressures, we could drum up the courage in Washington to use advertising as we need to use it.

Tuesday : . . December 22

Compared the results from a piece of mail order copy run in a publication printed on news stock and in another printed on m. f. book. Found that they had produced at almost exactly the same rate per thousand of circulation. But the lower page rate made possible by the newsprint made a great difference in the net to the advertiser. There is a good deal of evidence that, from the advertiser's point of view, the improvements in printing processes have made the quality of stock used in a publication of less importance than is commonly thought. At least, that the basic rate to reach a thousand people is of more importance.

Wednesday . . . December 23

Talked with an agent who, until the recent order abolishing enlistments, handled one of the paid campaigns for the armed forces. This program, he told me, was handled with no more difficulty than an ordinary commercial account. It went through with speed and efficiency and got results. In contrast, every agent I have talked with who has handled one of the voluntary jobs for government has had the same experience I have had: confusion much confounded. It is the efficiency of advertising which is at stake in the question of who pays for it.

Thursday . . . December 24

The Christmas cards are simpler this year, which is as it should be. But I would not like to see them discontinued, and hope that Uncle Sam will never have to ask us to do so. After the tree is decorated, and the house has quieted down, I like to sit and savor these greetings—especially those from the old friends whom I too seldom get to see or to hear from. It is the next best thing to having a wee dram together on Christmas Eve.

Friday . . . December 25

On an airport bus yesterday I met up with four
young lieutenants of the Army air forces. They
were sadly contemplating their first Christmas away
from home, in a city where they knew not a soul.
To make matters worse, their pay had not caught
up with them for two months, and they were practically strapped. So they accepted an invitation to
dinner today with alacrity. I have never seen a finer
bunch of boys. And God help the enemy if they
dive bomb him as they did our proud turkey from
the farm.

Saturday . . . December 26

The insatiable rollers of the presses are no re-
specters of holidays. So having an unfinished piece
of copy which had to be ready early next week, I
sat down at home to work at it. Now, I pride myself on my ability to concentrate on the typewriter
in almost any surroundings, but this time I went
down to defeat when the song of the vacuum
cleaner began in the land. Mr. Hoover should recommend it to women who also want to get a husband from under foot.

Sunday . . . December 27

Bethought myself that this column would reach
whatever readers it may have gathered on the first
business day of the New Year. So let me say, in the

words of Rip Van Winkle: "Here's to your good health, and the good health of your family. May you live long and prosper."

Monday . . . December 28

A letter from an English advertiser informs me that the old controversy about the agency commission method of compensation has flared up there. This seems a strange time for this hardy perennial to rear its head. As usual, the heart of the question is the advertiser's feeling that he is really the one who should determine the agent's rate of pay. Unfortunately, behind all of the "reason" and "principles" which are developed in debates on this subject, it always appears that the advertiser is saying to the agent, "Come work exclusively for me, and I will pay you less." Somehow or other this has never had much appeal to the agent.

Tuesday . . . December 29

Sat all day with a client, trying to help him plan a budgeted manufacturing and selling program for his spring season. Only three problems presented themselves. First, how to get enough raw materials to keep up his normal volume. Second, how to retain or train enough labor to convert these materials into finished goods. Third, how to provide management when he, himself, would probably be drafted before midyear. Aside from this everything was rosy.

95

Lunched with a former advertising man who is now a partner in a firm of business management consultants. He finds in such work full scope for use, at the management level, of all the analytical and creative techniques which advertising taught him. I was encouraged to learn that he now finds among his clients a very active interest in studies looking toward post-war plans. Only as such studies are made now, in every company, to plan for full employment at high levels, do I see any hope of avoiding the imposition of a state-planned economy.

Thursday . . . December 31

In a club, at lunch time, ran into a former client, who was already well under way on his New Year's celebration. For the twenty-five years or more that I have known this man he has been both a drunkard and a lecher, yet he and his business have flourished like the green bay tree. Pondering on this, I remembered how the prophet Jeremiah had once pleaded with the Lord to tell him, Why do the wicked prosper? And received no answer.

January, 1943

Friday . . . January 1

Who can begin this year without the solemn feeling that it is pregnant with decisions on the greatest issues in history? In this twelve months to come millions now living and generations yet unborn will have their fates determined. Both nations and races will have the outlines of their futures drawn. Before our very eyes the greatest drama of all time will be played.

Saturday . . . January 2

Over an illicit second cup of coffee at breakfast I scanned the want ads in a big city newspaper. I know of nothing which reflects more accurately the state of the nation in certain aspects. Here, for instance, is an index of the growing shortage of manpower, in the allurements held out to women to enter industry—a signal of the near-revolution in home life that is coming. Even the little nuances of the times can be picked up in these ads: as when one company calls itself "the Arsenal of Communications" to satisfy workers that here they can make a direct war contribution.

Sunday . . . January 3

In some fields of work knowledge is exact: for instance, where it is based on the *count* of things, as in the number of lines in a magazine page. In some other fields only approximate exactness may be attained; for instance, in the *measurement* of things to the nearest foot, inch, or thousandth of an inch. In still other fields knowledge is still intuitive, or at the best an appraisal of *probabilities*. What then is the nature of advertising knowledge? This is a question I have long tried to come to grips with, unsuccessfully. Decided this day to try to put down, every week, some notes on this subject, with the hope that I may eventually clarify it to myself.

Monday . . . January 4

Talked with a friend who has been plugging away for some years at the promotion of better relations with Latin America. He wonders why it is this subject never really captures the imagination of our people. I think it is because the tides of world history and of thought have always flowed east and west, never north and south. In such intangible forces does the fate of enterprises sometimes lie.

Tuesday . . . January 5

Advertising is something you pay for; publicity something you cadge for. How strange that this

98

somehow makes publicity more respectable than advertising—not only in government, but in some business quarters.

Wednesday . . . January 6

Studied the results of a careful consumer investigation in over 2,000 cross-section homes, on the use of two competing products. These two products, while very similar in their qualities, have long been advertised for somewhat different uses. In home after home, the report showed, both products were on hand—but each was confined to the uses for which it had been most featured. I have never seen more convincing evidence of the direct power of advertising to determine people's habits.

Thursday . . . January 7

Heard a professor defined as "a man who spends his life teaching people how to solve problems which he has spent most of his life escaping by becoming a professor." This is one of those witticisms which has just enough truth in it to get by. When some hundred economists are reported to have signed a petition to government for the elimination of advertising in war time, one may think all professors live in a dream world. But when it is remembered that most products now advertised can ultimately be traced back to some scientist's research, the little truth in such a remark becomes evident.

Friday . . . January 8

Sitting around in a bull session with a number of publishers, advertising agents, and advertisers, somebody asked for guesses on the total volume of national advertising in 1943. I ventured the estimate that it would be about the same as, or a little better than, last year. Other estimates ranged down from this to a 10% loss. The leading publisher of magazines present believed that it would be about 10% up for the first six months, 10% down for the last six months, or about even for the year.

Saturday . . . January 9

Began the reading of the new life of Willard Gibbs, the comparatively unknown man who Einstein says had one of the most original and creative scientific minds America has produced. His story reminded me of the saying that the human being has three basic hungers: the hunger of the belly, the hunger of the loins, and the hunger of the mind. Gibbs had the last of these in such remarkable degree that, in his attempts to satisfy it, he changed the scientific thinking of the entire world.

Sunday . . . January 10

ON THE NATURE OF ADVERTISING KNOWLEDGE. The old correspondence school ads used to say that Knowledge is Power. Power to do what? Does it not come down to the power to

100

predict what will happen? We "know" that 2 plus 2 makes 4, because every time we have added 2 things to 2 other things we have found we had 4 things; so we safely predict that it will happen again. We "know" that the rate in a certain publication is, say, $10,000 a page, because we can reliably predict that we will get a bill for this amount if we use it. Knowledge then, in advertising or elsewhere, is the power to predict. To the extent that we lack that power we lack knowledge. What an area of ignorance that leaves in advertising!

Monday . . . January 11

The latest retirement of A. D. Lasker from the agency business reminds me of a talk I once had with him about it. He said there were only three things of major importance which had ever happened in the history of that business. The first was when F. W. Ayer, with his original contract, made it a business. The second was when he, Lasker, hired John Kennedy, paid him $28,000 a year, and dramatized copy as the most important element in the business. The third was when J. Walter Thompson Company introduced sex into advertising, in "The Skin You Love to Touch."

Tuesday . . . January 12

Talked with one of our high officials who has an intimate knowledge of the Russians. Asked him why we were not permitted military observers on the

Russian front. The answer, he said, is very simple: the Russians have secret agents in every department in Washington. Knowing how easy it is to place them there, they assume that the Germans have them, too. Thus they figure that reports from their front would sooner or later fall into German hands. I was so astounded I forgot to ask why we couldn't stop this.

Wednesday . . . January 13

Reading a book on semantics called "Language in Action" I ran across this for advertising people to think about: "The reader may say, 'If people want to pay for daydreams in their bath salts and want to battle imaginary diseases with imaginary cures, isn't that their business?' It isn't entirely. The willingness to rely on words instead of examining facts is a disorder in the communicative process . . . And it doesn't seem beyond the bounds of possibility that today's suckers for national advertising will be tomorrow's suckers for the master political propagandist who will, by playing up the 'Jewish menace' in the same way as national advertisers play up the 'pink tooth-brush menace', and by promising us national glory in the same way as national advertisers promise us personal glory and prosperity, sell fascism in America."

Thursday . . . January 14

The two most important facts in the advertising business today are these: First, that the government

102

seems politically unable to buy the space which is badly needed for a score or more of home front jobs. Second, that millions of dollars' worth of space is still being used in self-glorification or sentimental bellywash by advertisers with no goods to sell. If some way is not found to mobilize this space for much needed public service it may be an everlasting discredit to this business.

Friday . . . January 15

Most of the men I talk with these days are worrying about how to do more in the war effort. They have an uneasy feeling that they are only yielding to self-interest when told that they can actually serve best by staying in their jobs. But today I had the unpleasant experience of dealing with a man who hardly seemed to know there was a war going on. I was offering him a job for which he seemed eminently fitted, which would be wholly in the public service, but in which he could be well paid. Finding that the public service side of it had no appeal to him whatsoever, I decided he was not fitted for the job after all, and withdrew the offer.

Saturday . . . January 16

For the first time in weeks managed to get in a day at the farm. The roads to it are rough with frozen ruts, and what with this and the gas rationing, the folks there don't get out much, so they were very glad to see me. But the radio keeps them up to the minute on all that the world is doing and failing to do, and I found them as keen in their discussions of current affairs as any of my city friends —and a lot more sane and salty.

Sunday . . . January 17

ON THE NATURE OF ADVERTISING KNOWLEDGE. Most of us got such scientific education as we have in the days when the scientist's whole emphasis was on the search for cause and effect. Therefore, in such efforts as we have made to develop a science of advertising we have sought cause-effect sequences—with very meager results. Now that scientists like Einstein have shown that even in the physical world there are too many causes and too many effects for such a simple formula, we may get a more productive point of view. The laws of probability, which are now recognized by physicists as well as by gamblers, are likely to be much nearer to our problems.

Monday . . . January 18

Talking with a new client who has suddenly discovered copy testing, I found the usual over-expectation of quick results from such procedures. A consistent program of such testing can be productive, and lead to improvements in copy. But such a program requires an infinite patience, a willingness to test and re-test, and an ability to suspend judgments

104

which most promotion-minded people do not seem to have.

Tuesday . . . January 19

Placed an order today for the insertion of a proven mail order page in a publication not previously used, and told the representative how many units of merchandise it would have to sell to pay. He nearly fainted. Most publication people believe in advertising in the same way that they believe in God—that it "moves in mysterious ways its wonders to perform." They really wince when they see this mystery about to be subjected to the cold test of traceable results. Apparently they have too little genuine conviction that the printed page can be made to sell—right now.

Wednesday . . . January 20

Publishers to whom the recent cut in paper tonnage presents a difficult problem should review their ideas about the kind of paper they have to use. No doubt in the competitive selling of one publication against another the kind of paper may be important. But actually, so far as advertising response is concerned, I can find very little evidence that the kind of paper has anything to do with the effectiveness of the message. "The Kid in Upper Four" will get a reading on newsprint as quickly as it will on m. f. book or coated stock.

105

Thursday . . . January 21

There are all sorts of devices of layout and illustration which will improve the reading ratings of ads. But if you want to make sure of flagging the attention of the most *prospects* don't overlook the appeal of the merchandise itself. Most of us are natural window shoppers at any time. But when we are *in the market* then the merchandise or a picture of it is the best stopper.

Friday . . . January 22

Going through a big city newspaper my eye picked up an obscure item with a date line from my home town. I have had this happen again and again. In fact, I will pick up the name of this town, and focus on it, when it is buried in the middle of a newspaper story over which my eye is merely roaming. This suggests that getting "attention" is far more a matter of what you say than it is of the size space you say it in. In short, it is doubtful whether "attention," like the Kingdom of Heaven, can be taken by force. The reasons for using large space are of other kinds.

Saturday . . . January 23

Had a report from Washington that the New Dealers are plotting to have OPA use its powers to establish government grade labeling for many kinds of merchandise. This might well be opposed on the ground of the huge army of graders that would be called for, but otherwise I cannot get excited about it. Unless private branding is abolished altogether, both the pros and the antis on this subject will find that the public will pay very little attention to these grades, and that consumer preferences for brands can still be maintained.

Sunday . . . January 24

ON THE NATURE OF ADVERTISING KNOWLEDGE. I have a friend who used to say that only God Almighty Himself is really equipped to be an advertising man. What he meant was that the mere number of subjects and skills in which we need mastery is impressive, and beyond a lifetime's encompassment. I have tried listing them, and find that they would make a four-year school curriculum comparable to that for a doctor's or lawyer's degree.

Monday . . . January 25

Wakened early by the clop-clop of a horse's hoofs coming down our city street, followed by the rattle of milk bottles. Thought for a moment I was back in my boyhood, in that automobileless world which the generation after mine cannot even picture. Later in the day I talked with a taxi driver who was bemoaning his inability to get any recreation, now that he couldn't drive for pleasure. Told him how I used to ride with my girl on a streetcar, to the city limits, and then take a walk in the country. He was appalled at the notion.

Tuesday . . . January 26

Thinking about my friend the taxi driver, above, I was reminded of that amazing man, H. G. Wells. In the early days of this century he wrote a book with the longest title I ever remember seeing. It was called "Anticipations of the Reactions from Mechanical and Scientific Progress upon Human Life and Thought." In it—and this was before the automobile had changed our lives—he described the coming of a new type of individual of whom my taxi driver is a perfect example. It would be interesting to check that book now and see how many other of his anticipations came true.

Wednesday . . . January 27

Sat around all evening with a group of younger industrialists who were discussing the post-war world. I was pleasantly surprised at the freshness of their views. The old bleats about private enterprise and the New Deal were conspicuous by their absence. In their place was serious discussion of the planning business itself had to do to meet the new demands of people for a world of both material and psychological satisfactions. Very hopeful.

Thursday . . . January 28

See by the papers that Bill Benton is now going to run the Encyclopaedia Britannica for the University of Chicago, in addition to his other duties there.

Bill is a pretty smart hombre. He often rushes in where angels fear to tread—and comes out with golden wings. But this one is going to tax his ingenuity. If he can forget that he is now an educator, and remember that an encyclopaedia is part of the furniture industry, he may pull it off.

Friday . . . January 29

Talked with a publisher who told me that, in his opinion, the cuts in paper tonnage have just begun, and that there will be other and more serious ones before the year is out. The English experience with this, which has been severe, is that the process is very painful until the necessary adjustments are made, after which it does not work out too badly. Now that we are in for it, the creative people in the agencies had better start dusting off their almost forgotten talents for making small space do a job.

Saturday . . . January 30

No chance to get to the farm today because of deep snow blocking all the roads. So betook myself to the seed catalogs, and with paper and pencil began to lay out an enlarged Victory garden. Sometimes I think the best part of a farm is the time you don't spend there. Then you can forget how the septic tank fails to work at the most inconvenient moments, and concentrate on that Shangri-La in which all the masterpieces of horticulture flourish, and the jug at the end of the furrow is full of nectar.

109

ON THE NATURE OF ADVERTISING KNOWLEDGE. Received a fine, thoughtful letter on this subject from my old friend, Marco Morrow, with which I am in essential agreement. But I would make my own classification of his points in some such way as this: First come facts; or, as the scientist says, data. These are only the raw materials of knowledge. When education is limited to these then we get, as Marco points out, a "learned fool." Second comes knowledge, that is, the synthesis of and inductions from facts, leading to general principles and to directives for getting things done. Third comes wisdom—the appraisal of knowledge in the light of values—which tells us what is worth doing with our knowledge. Whitehead's introduction to "Business Adrift," long a favorite of mine, is a perfect example of knowledge distilled into wisdom.

February, 1943

Monday . . . February 1

Some of the old-time fighting newspaper editors like Fremont Older, who turned San Francisco upside down, knew how to conduct campaigns that would develop social pressures. But today's newspaper men, especially the better ones, are a different breed of cats. Their whole training disposes them (1) to think of each story as hot today and cold tomorrow; (2) to be as objective and free from persuasion in their reporting as possible; (3) to look upon ad men as scum from the business office who are always trying to corrupt editorial virtue. No wonder these men have failed so miserably to understand their job in Washington. As propagandists they are pitiful in their limitations.

Tuesday . . . February 2

Speaking of Fremont Older reminds me of the day I called upon him when a big ad of mine had just appeared in his paper. He said he thought it was one of the most striking and interesting he had ever seen. I asked him if he also thought it was believable, and would make people want the product advertised. He saw the point at once, but said it was one which had not occurred to him before—that an advertisement could be interesting without selling anything. It doesn't seem to occur today to many who fasten their eyes too exclusively on reading ratings.

Wednesday . . . February 3

The anonymity of this Diary seems to be wearing a bit thin. Twice today I was accused of keeping it. Under similar circumstances Boswell records that the famous Dr. Johnson once said, in effect, that any man who is so imprudent as to attempt the invasion of a desired privacy of this kind should expect to be lied to.

Thursday . . . February 4

Herb Verst, publisher of the *Wholesale Grocer News*, sends me an article analyzing the idea now abroad that, in the future society, a minimum of free food for all may seem just as logical as a minimum of free schooling for all does now. This is the kind of discussion we need, pro and con, of all these ideas. One of the old posers of the philosophers used to be, Can the world be *thought* out or must it be *fought* out? The idea that it can be thought out is a totalitarian one, beloved of planners. The counter idea that it must be fought out is the democratic one. As long as Herb can raise his voice in debate we are safe.

112

Friday . . . February 5

The Washington administrators have my sympathy. This economy of ours is so complex a machine that hardly any move can be made to adjust one part of it to war without throwing another unobserved part out of gear. The Manpower Commission, for example, has raised a dither in every advertising agency office this week by its pronouncement on the draft of married men. But almost at the same time Gardner Cowles of OWI re-affirms his position that his office must rely upon advertisers and their agents to carry a big part of the load on the informational front. As Hamlet might have said: "To be or not to be—essential; that is the question."

Saturday . . . February 6

Pleased to read this morning of the selection of Chet LaRoche as Advertising Man of the Year, for his work as leader of the Advertising Council. I must admit that I was suspicious of the Council, when it first started, as just another of those fifth wheels which the "joiners" of this world are always putting together. But having had some opportunity to see what it has accomplished behind the scenes in Washington, as well as in print and on the air, I am now convinced that the Council has become the most useful and important organization in advertising.

113

ON THE NATURE OF ADVERTISING
KNOWLEDGE. The educators now tend to class-
ify the different "subjects" of the older college
courses into four fields of knowledge: namely, the
physical sciences, the biological sciences, the social
sciences, and the humanities. The great advances in
knowledge in the past hundred years have been in
the physical and biological sciences. These in turn
have made possible great advances in the applica-
tions of these sciences in industry and medicine.
But advertising is an application of the social sciences. The lag in the development of "pure" science in this field is at the root of all our problems.

Monday . . . February 8

When I see a publication representative these
days I am reminded of that old limerick about the
young lady of Niger who went for a ride on a tiger.
As I recall it, they came back from the ride with
the lady inside—and a smile on the face of the tiger.
With the sellers' market which many publications
now enjoy, thanks to the paper shortage, the space
buyer who too often took representatives for a ride
now confronts a tigerish smile which is awful to
behold.

Tuesday . . . February 9

Listening to our new business man make a presentation to a prospective client, I thought how

114

badly this whole procedure of advertiser-agency selection is conducted. Too often both advertiser and agency put the emphasis on the wrong things. The difficulty is, of course, that the things which really count for an advertiser in agency service are hard for him to put his finger on and hard for the agency to exhibit. They lie almost wholly in the quality of the agency's thinking, vision, and courage. The process of examining or exhibiting an agency part by part, in all its mechanics, tends to evaporate all these really important qualities on which the advertiser should make his judgment— just as the petal by petal dissection of a flower destroys its bloom and perfume.

Wednesday . . . February 10

Thinking of post-war planning in terms of the advertising business itself, I began today to get up to date on the technical situation affecting future broadcasting. My first explorations brought me up with a jerk. If what the technicians say is true, there is a revolution impending, once the war is over, in the now possible developments of television, frequency modulation, and the transmission of graphics.

Thursday . . . February 11

Today, after many years, I met a friend of my youth who used to be an ardent socialist, filled with visions of reforming the world. He says he never got over it until he married and found how difficult it is to change just one woman. From a close study along similar lines, I have often wondered how we manage to make enough converts to make advertising pay.

Friday . . . February 12

Dining in a small, quiet restaurant in New York last night I discovered that the proprietor had once been cook, butler, and houseman for George Buckley, in the days when George was president of the Crowell Publishing Co. Discovered, too, that for him as for me, George has never died. To this day I can see and hear him as he was the first time I met him—when he walked into my office and said he had come West to look for an ad writer who "knew how a manure pile smells on a frosty morning."

Saturday . . . February 13

Sat me down in the Saturday morning quiet to turn out an overdue piece of copy. First came those two or three false starts, like the cranking of a cold engine. Then a phrase came through with a spark, and the mental engine raced for a minute and died. Then a new start, but this time with more confidence that the juice was there. A little adjustment of the carburetor, so to speak—to sixteen parts gas and one part hot air—and soon I was purring along to the end of the run. Nothing like it.

116

Sunday . . . February 14

ON THE NATURE OF ADVERTISING
KNOWLEDGE. Among the "pure" sciences of
which advertising is an application are individual
psychology, social psychology, sociology, economics, and linguistics. For example, there are some
studies in social psychology which indicate that individuals break down old habits and acquire new
ones most readily in times of mass crisis. Today is
such a time. Thus these studies suggest that there
is more danger to old brand habits, and more opportunity for new ones now than in normal times.

Monday . . . February 15

I wonder if these maps of the shrinking world
which the airlines are publishing do not have a special significance for us advertising men. It was no
accident that the first advertising agents, such as
Rowell, Thompson, and Ayer, began their careers
coincident with the expansion of railroads in this
country. It was the shrinking of this continent by
steam transportation which made national distribution, national media, and national advertising possible. Another such development in the international field portends and the foreign editions of
Time and *Reader's Digest* are the forerunners of it.

Tuesday . . . February 16

Received today from a museum a series of very
beautiful color reproductions of objects of art in

their collection, done in a process which I could not identify. Upon investigation found they were produced by a comparatively new method called the photographic silk screen process. It gives much greater fidelity to the original than does four-color printing, and is inexpensive enough to use for jobs where only a short run is needed.

Wednesday . . . February 17

Watching one of our women writers present some of her work to a client today I thought what a mistake it was not to have had her do it before. Both writer and client gain from such a contact. The writer comes out of it with a much greater sense of the commercial realities of the problem; and the client gets a much greater appreciation of the real thought and work which has been put into what is proposed to him.

Thursday . . . February 18

Woke at three this morning with a full-fledged idea for one client's next campaign. Long ago I learned to shoot these nocturnal birds on the wing, and to keep pad and pencil by my bedside to do it with. So propped myself up in bed and went to work to get the idea on paper. By five I was able to turn out the light and put both the conscious and unconscious minds back into deep dreams of peace.

118

Friday . . . February 19

Attended the meeting in New York at which representatives of the government and the Advertising Council placed some of their major information problems before the food industry. This will come close to being the critical test of OWI's declared intention to rely on private industry for its advertising needs. In spite of some deficiencies in the presentations at this meeting, the proposals were, on the whole, well received by the advertisers present. Now let us see how well they will implement them.

Saturday . . . February 20

Put in some hours weeding my overcrowded bookshelves to see what I might contribute to the Victory Books campaign. The task turned out to be a sort of sentimental journey through all my yesterdays, as I picked up and looked into books which I had not handled for years. Here was one which, as a young man, had the most profound influence on me of any book I ever read. Here were gifts from acquaintances almost forgot; *memorabilia* of journeys long ago made; signposts of intellectual byways started down and never followed. And here, too, I regret to say, were books borrowed in forgotten days and never returned. A pretty good picture of a man's life, his bookshelves.

Sunday . . . February 21

ON THE NATURE OF ADVERTISING
KNOWLEDGE. How much can the workers in
psychology of the individual contribute to advertising? The record is not clear. Walter Dill Scott, I
believe, made the first attempt more than twenty-
five years ago, in his "Psychology of Advertising,"
with meager results. Later the famous exponent of
Behaviorism, John Watson, tried his hand at it. But
advertising absorbed John without absorbing much
of his psychology. Recently a friend of mine reported some productive results from the use of
techniques developed by Freud. But on the whole,
I am inclined to look to the work of the social psy-
chologists as more likely to bear fruit which we can
pick.

Monday . . . February 22

Working at home on this holiday, I was run down
on the long distance phone by a client in an area
where Washington's birthday is not observed. In
our concentration on national advertising and marketing we sometimes overlook how strong the re-
gional influences still are in this vast country. One
example of them is the variation in the observance
of Lincoln's and Washington's birthdays. In it can
be traced not only the old Civil War lines of cleav-
age, but other variations in political thinking and
customs which influence people's behavior.

120

Tuesday . . . February 23

Over the entire week-end and holiday just passed I not only worked at home myself, but had several other people doing the same, in order to complete a job of writing which a client had said *must* be ready today. Now, upon delivery, it turns out that he cannot consider using it for several weeks. One reason why copywriters quietly go mad.

Wednesday . . . February 24

A St. Louis correspondent wants to know what I would suggest as post-war discussion material for a small group of business men who are exploring this subject together. I would strongly recommend, first, that they read and discuss Peter Drucker's two books: "The End of Economic Man" and "The Future of Industrial Man." After that, I would get all of the material issued by the Committee for Economic Development, and see how I could help implement the plans of this committee, locally. This latter material may be had by writing the committee at the Commerce Building, Washington.

Thursday . . . February 25

The item above reminds me of the night I attended the meeting of a somewhat similar group in London, some years ago. This was composed of about 20 able men from various walks of life. They met once a month, for a dutch treat dinner, and informal discussion over pipes and ale afterward. Each meeting was devoted to some one subject, with the discussion started by a man who knew something about it. The night I was there the subject was Euthanasia, or legalized mercy deaths by doctors, which was then being proposed in a bill before Parliament. The exponent was the head of one of London's big hospitals, and the leading opponent a Church of England priest. We need more such groups in this country, to take the place of the old cracker barrel forums, and to bring us individually into contact with people outside our own trade and social groups.

Friday . . . February 26

A couple of years ago a brilliant but shy woman came to enlist my interest in a social service enterprise which she believed was much needed. She wanted to work for its development herself, but wanted somebody else to take the leadership. When I urged her to carry the banner herself she said she had no capacity for it. I told her just to make a start, and then keep putting one foot in front of another. She did, and today I had the pleasure of seeing her dream completed. Thus are great things done.

Saturday . . . February 27

Worked on my farm income tax report, and suddenly, through all the tedious computations, began to feel the sap of the farm's life. Here was the record of plowing, planting, and harvesting; of breeding, feeding, and marketing. Here were the successes and the failures—and the men who shared in them, with their sweat, their jokes, their friendships. When the tax collector comes, can spring be far behind?

Sunday . . . February 28

ON THE NATURE OF ADVERTISING KNOWLEDGE. One of the old debates among the philosophers is whether the world should be viewed as a collection of separate individuals, or whether society in the aggregate is a sort of thing-in-itself. That is, are there just a lot of separate minds to be influenced, or is there a super mass-mind? Now this is, in fact, the debate which is at the root of two different schools of advertising thought. For example, the mail order advertiser usually seems to think of the world as a collection of individuals, each of which he is trying to sell separately. At the other extreme, the so-called institutional advertiser usually seems to have hazy ideas about influencing the mass-mind. Not only copy styles are affected by which of these views is held, but the choice of media may be determined by it.

March, 1943

Monday . . . March 1

Lunched with a well-known economist. He claimed that the greatest war danger to which the American people are not yet awake is inflation. In England, he said, this has been stopped in its tracks by taxes and enforced savings, and by complete wage and price controls. He thought our government would never have the courage to go as far until the people were aroused to the danger. Here is a theme some advertisers may see a chance to do something with.

Tuesday . . . March 2

Looking over a series of rough layouts submitted by an art director today, I wondered how we came to make this end of our business so complex. The straining that goes on for originality in layout is mostly hocus-pocus. If we would only stick to the simple, direct, and unself-conscious forms that are really the best we could materially reduce the cost of ad preparation. Perhaps the growing shortage of art directors will teach us this.

124

Wednesday . . . March 3

The Army has a good many so-called public relations officers, but the increasing questioning of its policies makes me wonder whether they are up to their job. There may be the best reasons in the world why we need the size Army which the heads of it are demanding; and why they need to buy up all the great quantities of goods they are taking off the market; but if so the public has not been made to understand them. The greatest post-war tragedy that could happen to us would be such a revulsion from military ways as would throw us back into another starved Army program.

Thursday . . . March 4

Nine-tenths of all the waste work in this business comes from trying to write copy before we have really determined what it is we are trying to sell. The answer seems obvious when we have a product that we want the reader or listener to buy, but the *proposition* we are going to make him to get him to buy is not always so easy to formulate. And today, when so often we are trying to sell an idea only, the clear definition of that idea is a necessary prerequisite to good copy work.

Friday . . . March 5

Visiting in New York today I was invited to attend a meeting of the Advertising Council. It would

125

be my respectful suggestion to this group that it extend as many such invitations as is practicable. No one attending such a meeting can fail to be impressed by the evidences of the devoted and intelligent work which the Council is doing in the total war effort.

Saturday . . . March 6

Lunching with some friends in a smart restaurant, they pointed out to me the woman who is the "Blithe Spirit" in Noel Coward's play of that name. But I thought the real blithe spirit was at our table —a young woman living on what a lieutenant husband could send her, and suffused with happiness because she will soon be a mother.

Sunday . . . March 7

ON THE NATURE OF ADVERTISING KNOWLEDGE. One of the reasons why we need to get this subject fully developed, and its parts defined, is to be better able to say who is an advertising man. When we employ a lawyer, doctor, or even an architect we have the guarantee that he has been subjected to the learning of at least some minimum body of knowledge. I can see no reason why the business man, when he is invited to risk large sums of money on the judgment of an advertising man, should not have similar assurances.

Monday . . . March 8

Talked today with the owner of a small business which has been liquidated for lack of materials and labor. It was not a business of any particular importance to its community, and it seemed a very dull one to outsiders. But it was this man's "work of art," the thing that gave meaning to his life. For twelve years he had struggled to build it up, putting into it all his money, all his energies, and all his dreams. Probably no big corporation employe, from president down, can ever understand how much more than a livelihood this man has lost.

Tuesday . . . March 9

It seems to me that I have never seen a time when our clients made so many demands upon us for overnight work. The exigencies of their own war adaptations, plus the unforeseen demands from government for assistance, are, of course, at the bottom of it. Coming on top of our own growing manpower shortages these demands wreck all efforts at production scheduling, and run our overtime into fantastic figures. Some days I feel we are entitled to put up that motto of General Somervell's: "We do the Impossible immediately; the Miraculous takes a little longer."

Wednesday . . . March 10

It wasn't too long ago that even the best advertising illustrators of the country were crying for work.

Photography and "realism" were the order of the day, and the art director who proposed using anything else was eyed askance and suspected of being out-of-date. Now all this is changed. Campaign after campaign built around the painted picture breaks into print. The illustrators are in the saddle again, and art directors run at their stirrups. Youngsters in the business might make note of this as one of those fashion cycles in advertising which they will often see repeated in their lifetime.

Thursday . . . March 11

Talked with several of the big food processors who had been called to Washington and asked by Secretary Wickard to raise a fund of $2,500,000 to do an urgent advertising job for him. They were all hopping mad about it, and the Secretary was poorly advised to handle it in the way he did. But what the food men overlook is one highly significant fact in this request. This is, I think, the first time that a high ranking member of this administration has expressed a dependence upon advertising to get his job done. And that is very important to an industry which in turn is as dependent upon advertising as the food industry is.

Friday . . . March 12

Thirty years ago I had something to do with the introduction of one of the first products for checking and deodorizing perspiration. Shortly thereafter the *Journal of the American Medical Association* pilloried it as a dangerous preparation; and Samuel Hopkins Adams, in a series of muckraking articles, cited it as a flagrant example of the harm done to the public by ad men. Indeed, for many years the whole field of personal grooming preparations has been a happy hunting ground for the advertising reformer. But now the War Production Board lists deodorants and other cosmetics as among the essentials of a bedrock economy; and the most hard-bitten industrial managers have suddenly discovered what color, clothes, and cosmetics mean to the morale of women workers. Thus does Time confound the views of men.

Saturday . . . March 13

Had an interesting discussion today, with an advertiser, about the level of public taste. He belongs to the school which believes that good taste in advertising is an actual deterrent to sales; that, like Tiffany's windows, it makes the average man or woman feel "this is not for me." He also cites the way most people dress and furnish their homes as proof that their appreciation of color and form is at a low level. But I contended that there has been a great improvement in the public taste in the last generation; and that in the average person the appreciation of beauty exceeds his ability to create it. I think one proof of this change may be found in a comparison of the mail order catalogs of today with those of twenty years ago.

Sunday . . . March 14

ON THE NATURE OF ADVERTISING
KNOWLEDGE. The physical sciences have made
their great advances through the experimental
method. The biological sciences likewise. But the
social sciences (of which advertising is an application) have been woefully handicapped because
their problems cannot be brought under the same
degree of experimental control. As a substitute
technique these sciences have turned to new methods in statistics, so that more and more it looks as
though the advertising man of the future will have
to learn the language of the higher mathematics.
A dreary outlook.

Monday . . . March 15

Busied myself with the final details of getting off
my income tax report, and then sat up late solacing
myself with an intriguing book called "Life in a
Noble Household 1641-1700." It shows how the first
Duke of Bedford got and spent his income, down
to the last pence. If our income tax reports called
for the same kind of detailed report the country
would probably revolt—but we would have the
greatest body of marketing data possible to secure.

Tuesday . . . March 16

Interested to note the appearance recently of institutional and financial report advertisements from
two proprietary medical houses. In the days when

130

Earl Reeve was the star salesman for *The Saturday Evening Post* in the West he used to refer to certain kinds of promotion as "confidential advertising." By this he meant advertising which might be highly effective as a direct selling tool, but which failed to build any over-all reputation for the company. Medical advertisers, by and large, have always hewed to this line; but every man yearns for some kind of public recognition sooner or later.

Wednesday . . . March 17

In came a client with his bowels in an uproar because a competitor had been allowed to make some exaggerated claims in a recent publication. Such things, of course, are worth keeping an eye on, and making proper protests about. But in the long run I always think Willie Hoppe had the right idea. When somebody asked his manager how it was that Willie always won his matches, the answer was: "Willie is always playing billiards, while his competitors are always playing Willie."

Thursday . . . March 18

Heard on good authority that the Army is barely keeping up with its need for blood plasma. This modern miracle is saving so many lives on the battlefields that I began to wonder why more people, including myself, had not contributed their pint of blood. Made a little first-hand investigation which indicated that most people shrunk from the idea

131

because the simple procedure they would have to go through was unknown. When this was explained, specifically and in detail, their squeamishness tended to disappear. To get a man to do a thing, let him see himself doing it.

Friday . . . March 19

The incredible fact that America, the nation of plenty, can be short of food, is now coming home to every man's table. Six months ago I heard one of the leaders of the food industry warn a group of top people in Washington that this would happen, but they paid no attention to him. Now we are in for it, and probably Secretary Wickard, as Food Administrator, will get the blame. But the truth is that this is another case of divided responsibility—Manpower Commission on farm labor, WPB on farm machinery, OPA on price controls, and Army and Lease-Lend on purchasing policies.

Saturday . . . March 20

Went to see Helen Hayes in her new part as Harriet Beecher Stowe. When I got home, could not rest until I had searched out a yellowed copy of "Uncle Tom's Cabin," given me in 1896 by a long-forgotten teacher. Found I remembered the story clearly enough, but had not been conscious of the way it was interlarded with discussion and denunciation of the slave traffic. Badly written though it is, here is one of the most influential tracts ever produced, and we advertising men can learn something from it.

Sunday . . . March 21

ON THE NATURE OF ADVERTISING KNOWLEDGE. What about Prestige—that intangible quality which is over and above merit or authority, and is so valuable to a product or company when secured? What are the ways in which advertising can help build it? There is a story about Lord Chesterfield which is suggestive. "Walk down the street with me," he said to a socially ambitious young man, "it will make your fortune." Thus, perhaps, do certain kinds of testimonials work—transferring prestige by association. But here is a whole field for study in itself.

Monday . . . March 22

Talked with a banker who has been making an intensive study of post-war prospects. He believes, as I do, that the strongest demand of the people of this country will be for full and continuous employment. The demand for this may be so strong that every business will have to plan its operations with such employment as its first objective. In such planning advertising will have to receive a new kind of consideration from top management, as one tool in a program for continuous production.

133

Tuesday . . . March 23

Two weeks ago a client notified me that he would have to go out of business because his draft board had notified him that his enterprise was nonessential, and that both he and his male employes must register with the U. S. Employment Service for essential occupations. Today he wired me that a new ruling had come through declaring his business essential to civilian supply. Respectfully referred to the advocates of a planned economy.

Wednesday . . . March 24

Darwin developed his great theory of evolution and the origin of species from his observation of the variations in plants and animals. Even minute variations, he found, often gave one variety a winning edge in the struggle for survival. Working in accordance with this law, plant and animal breeders nurture these minute variations until they develop dramatic improvements and even new species—as Luther Burbank did, for instance. The same law holds good for merchandise. Often the variations between competitive products are minute ones. But searched out and nurtured by advertising they become the basis for product survival, improvement, and development. This is why government grade labeling and other efforts at standardization are, in the long run, deterrents to progress.

134

Thursday . . . March 25

Rereading tonight one of Sir Francis Younghus-band's books on the attempts to climb Mt. Everest I was struck by one incident. At the last minute the Grand Llama of Tibet became suspicious of the motives of one expedition and refused it permission to climb the mountain. But the leader explained to him that his group belonged to a strange religious sect whose Gods lived on mountain tops. It was therefore necessary for his people to climb mountains for purposes of worship. This was putting the matter in a light which a religious leader like the Llama could understand, and permission was graciously accorded. Salesmanship.

Friday . . . March 26

Traveling once myself along the border of Tibet, I was offered by a furtive native trader a most beautiful hand-embroidered bedspread. It had been made, he said, for the bed of an Indian princess. He also implied that it might have been stolen therefrom. Doubtless the tale wasn't true, but it added an interest to the piece which raised its value in my eyes, and does to this day—so that whenever I exhibit it I tell this story. A subjective value, aided by good copy, which I cheerfully paid for.

Saturday . . . March 27

Got through to the farm, and found that the tulips which I planted last fall are up about three inches,

135

and the ground already turned for vegetable planting. The new chicken house is finished, for an increased production of eggs and fryers. Two steers are fattening for butchering as we need them, and the supply of hams and bacon will hold us until next fall. Appointed myself head of the Rationing Board.

Sunday . . . March 28

ON THE NATURE OF ADVERTISING KNOWLEDGE. J. B. S. Haldane, a famous English biochemist, was once urged to take an active part in politics. He replied that he was doing so by sticking to his laboratory and exploring the chemical foundations of human behavior. Explaining this, he said that a hundred years ago no metallurgist could tell a rule-of-thumb worker in steel anything that was as useful as the worker's "feel" for his material. But eventually the scientific worker in this field was able to revolutionize steel processing. So in politics, he thought, the practicing politician, with his intuitive knowledge, could beat the scientific student of human nature all hollow today; but that eventually the scientist would catch up and pass him. So it is in advertising. We must still make most decisions on an intuitive basis. But it is not smart to hold that there will never be any other basis, and to shut our eyes to the growing body of measurable knowledge as it develops.

136

Monday . . . March 29

Strolling along a New York canyon at sundown I noted for the first time that the skyscrapers of commerce reach nearer to Heaven than do the spires of the churches. Thought there must be some significance in this, but just what it was eluded me for the moment.

Tuesday . . . March 30

Interested in studying the reading ratings on two different publication campaigns which we have run on the same product. The first secured relatively high ratings, and was accompanied by a modest increase in sales. The second secured very low ratings, but was followed by a sensational sales increase. The conclusion seems to be that reading ratings are just what the name implies—good indicators of reading, but not necessarily indicators of the sales appeal of what is read.

Wednesday . . . March 31

Years ago I had a client who went from New York to Atlantic City for nearly every week-end. He insisted on having the railroad right of way practically lined with painted bulletins displaying his name and wares, the chief value of which was that he could sit in the club car with his friends and watch himself march by. Some of the easy war money of today is resulting in the same kind of advertising, particularly in publications read principally by business men.

137

April, 1943

Thursday . . . April 1

See by the trade news that another big advertiser has split his business among four agencies. If a manufacturer has products which are closely competitive between themselves—as in the soap business—I can see some wisdom in this procedure. But when an advertiser's chief reason for such a move is to maintain an alleged state of competition between agencies he makes a mistake. The failure to secure an over-all counseling relationship with one good agency will more than offset the possible gains from a competitive stimulus among agencies.

Friday . . . April 2

In Washington talked with some of the labor people who were riled over Lou Maxon's rise to power in OPA. It seems that Lou doubted whether grade labeling would be a factor in the winning of the war. This alone was enough to make Donald Montgomery, now CIO representative to OPA, cry "Off with his head!" These battles of the Potomac are great helps to Hitler.

138

Saturday . . . April 3

Woke at the farm to find a warm sun shining and every sour cherry tree a miracle of bloom. But by nightfall a cold wind came up out of the Northwest which made me shiver with apprehension for my future pies. Thanked the Lord that I had had sense enough to plant my orchard where there is good air drainage, so that my chances of being frosted out are greatly diminished.

Sunday . . . April 4

ON THE NATURE OF ADVERTISING KNOWLEDGE. It is said that a Lord & Thomas man once tried to persuade A. D. Lasker to set up a market research department. "What good would it do?" said A. D. "A stack of figures a foot high wouldn't change my mind if I didn't agree with them." This story may be apocryphal, but it perfectly illustrates the reliance which skilled advertising men have placed on their intuitions. Lasker had these intuitive processes highly developed, and used them with great profit to himself and his clients. What these processes are, and how they may be developed, are still subjects of the highest importance in our craft.

Monday . . . April 5

Went over several pieces of copy done by a competent writer. Everything about them was sound, but there was no magic in them—none of that intangible quality which makes one girl, or one piece of merchandise seem more desirable than all the rest. Telling a copywriter how to capture this is about as difficult as telling a wallflower how to do it.

Tuesday . . . April 6

Talked with a former ad man who is now a naval officer assigned to duty in Washington. He thought that most men who have gone there in uniform are happy, and most who have gone as civilian volunteers are unhappy. The difference, he said, is that the uniformed man learns to take orders, do the job he is assigned to as best he can, and let somebody else assume the responsibility for winning the war. He doesn't expect to do it all by himself, as the civilians do.

Wednesday . . . April 7

Being a believer in the long-run value of a properly run labor union, probably I shouldn't speculate on this thought. But as a technical problem in social pressures it has interested me to observe the maladroit procedures of the opponents of unions. The sure way to destroy unions would be to devise means of making them socially unpopular among the people they must appeal to. The fact that such groups as airline pilots and newspaper writers like to avoid the word "union" when they organize suggests that this might not be impossible.

140

Thursday . . . April 8

There is a good deal of talk nowadays about how the C and D economic groups have practically disappeared, as war wages have pushed them up into the B or even A levels. No doubt this is so as far as incomes are concerned. But it does not follow that the consumption patterns in these homes change as rapidly or as radically. Indeed, there is concrete evidence that they do not. The social-cultural strata tend to remain the same, and the desire and taste for certain kinds of merchandise do not automatically follow upon purchasing power.

Friday . . . April 9

Studying a case in which one piece of copy has been constantly repeated for about five years with great success, I wondered why there are not more like it. Certainly there is a good deal of evidence that, for certain types of products, this repetition of one winning advertisement is more productive than the usual practice of making every insertion a different one. Probably one deterrent is the agency's fear that they will not seem to be earning their commissions. A procedure which solves this is to keep one piece of proved copy going, but also to keep up a testing program in the search for a better piece.

Saturday . . . April 10

Got my first planting of peas, carrots, chard, radishes, and onions into the ground; and then sat back

141

on my haunches watching the neat rows as though the first shoots might appear at any moment.

Sunday . . . April 11

ON THE NATURE OF ADVERTISING KNOWLEDGE. The intuitive processes, which every advertising man has to rely upon in the absence of exact knowledge, are a kind of distillation of his mother-wit. He builds his success on a stock of almost unconscious knowledge about the ways people of every kind live, learn, yearn, and act. This he has soaked up from the social soil in which he was raised, and his limitations will tend to be the limitations of that soil—by geography, income groups, and cultural patterns. As he prospers his dangers begin. There is very little sustenance for the intuitions in the rich suburbs, big hotels, and exclusive clubs. How, as Kipling said, to "walk with Kings nor lose the common touch" becomes his problem.

Monday . . . April 12

See by the papers that Dad Stanton, gentleman of the old school, has left us. I well remember the first day he called upon me, thirty-odd years ago, representing *Century Magazine*. When I asked him how much circulation his book had he looked shocked. Nobody, he said, had ever asked him that question before. Indeed, he, himself, had never asked it of the publisher, because everybody knew that the *Century* reached all the best people. I never bought any space from him, but I always admired and respected him.

Tuesday . . . April 13

A man toils at his business year after year, and sees a thousand specific things from which he draws the generalized conviction that "this is the greatest business—or greatest product—of its kind in the world." Then he wants to transmit that same general conviction to the public through advertising. Too often he feels that this can be done if he only shouts his own generalization loud enough and long enough. He forgets the thousand specific things out of which his generalization grew, and is unable to see that the best way to transmit his conviction is to let the public reach the same conclusion from the same specific experiences. Institutional advertising, in particular, suffers from this common human tendency.

Wednesday . . . April 14

Somewhat related to the above is the desire of the inexperienced advertiser to "hit 'em in the eye," with layout, type, and illustrations—particularly with big pictures of the package. We have all had the experience of finding ourselves trying to make a foreigner understand us by raising our voice. A lot of advertising shows evidence of the same instinctive delusion. The problem is not to "hit 'em in the eye," but to hit 'em in the mind.

143

Thursday . . . April 15

Musing on the two preceding entries I thought how much misunderstanding there is about the whole subject of getting attention in advertising. It is often dealt with as though the problem were a purely physical or optical one—forcing the eye to light on the ad. The difficulty of doing this is greatly exaggerated, even for small ads on a newspaper page. The real problem is to turn the flash of optical or auditory exposure which you buy into instant *mental* attention, by what you say. Use optics to give the eye a chance to focus on your baited hook, yes. But worry and work over that bait.

Friday . . . April 16

The hullabaloo made by the resigning writers of OWI's domestic division does highlight the basic confusion in that organization's policies. In the President's directive setting up this agency the word "propaganda" does not appear. It is technically an "information" agency, and a legalistic argument can be made that it has no charter for the conduct of propaganda—at least on the home front. But the fact is that the home front needs propaganda. Not in the sense of deceit, as its opponents use the word; but in the original sense, as used by the Church, for the Propagation of the Faith. Elmer Davis wavers between his rightful dislike of propaganda in the deceit sense, and his somewhat dim awareness of its need in the Faith sense.

144

Saturday . . . April 17

When I left town this morning for the farm a warm, gentle rain was falling. Every townsperson I saw was bemoaning a wet week-end, but I could only feel the seeds in my garden beginning to stir, the thirsty fruit trees uncurling more roots, and the alfalfa fields sucking more nitrogen into the soil.

Sunday . . . April 18

ON THE NATURE OF ADVERTISING KNOWLEDGE. It was Owen D. Young, I believe, who spoke some years ago to a graduating class of his Alma Mater about the education of the intuition. Thus if we need any dignifying of this alleged feminine quality as important in business we have it. I have never run across any scientific attempt to analyze the intuitive process, but I suppose its foundation must be in close observation and attentive listening. We all know that the most revealing things about a man are often his little, unconscious actions. Probably we store up our observations of these in a series of intangible, unformulated impressions; put them together in our minds unconsciously; and then some day say we have a "hunch" that he is a so-and-so.

Monday . . . April 19

"Where is your kid now?" said an old advertising friend when I met him on the street today. "Flying an Army transport from Brazil to Africa and India,"

I said. "Tell him to look up my youngster at the airport in Saud Arabia, where he hops across the Red Sea," he replied. Just casual like.

Tuesday . . . April 20

Finished reading the life of George Washington Carver, the great Negro scientist. Damyankees in particular ought to read it if they would understand what the Negro race is up against, and what the South suffers from. But what most impressed me in this book was its indirect and unspoken tribute to the role of the business man. For more than a quarter century Carver made magnificent contributions to industrial and agricultural chemistry; but very little appears to have been done with them, for lack of an exploiting mind to put them to use.

Wednesday . . . April 21

Lunched with a publisher of subscription books who was full of sighs over the irony of events. Never in forty years of such publishing had he seen such an appetite for his sets as now exists. It would be easy, he said, to become a millionaire almost overnight, if there were only enough paper available to turn out all the sets he could sell.

Thursday . . . April 22

Boring into the history and records of a new client's operations, I could see that I finally embarrassed him by the number of questions to which he should have known the answers but didn't. I have never seen the business (including my own) with which this couldn't be done. The late J. O. McKinsey of Chicago once told me that his whole success as a business analyst was built on such questions, and that even the great U. S. Steel Corporation couldn't answer them. We can all profit by this kind of scrutiny from a detached observer.

Friday . . . April 23

It seems to me that radio script writers—many of whom have had no printed advertising experience —do not always sufficiently value the opening sentence in the commercial. The temptation to turn the dial, or close the mind, on a commercial is the same as the tendency to flip a magazine page. So that first sentence in the commercial has the same job to do as the headline in print: namely, to intrigue the interest. There used to be a local station program for a loan office in Chicago which had the trick. As the music faded, over the air came the voice of the announcer saying: "Do any of you need money?"

Saturday . . . April 24

Took the farm truck into town today for a spring overhauling, and to get a load of bran and chops for our milk cows. I have an uneasy feeling that if I ever figured out the true cost of producing our milk I would find it cheaper to drink champagne.

But my churn demands no ration points; and if a man has his own clabber pans and cottage cheese sack in the milk house he can view many food shortages with equanimity.

Sunday . . . April 25

ON THE NATURE OF ADVERTISING KNOWLEDGE. If an advertisement is to have any emotional tug it must, like any other work of art, sum up and highlight a certain area of human experience. The relation of this to scientific knowledge is well stated by Karl Pearson in "The Grammar of Science." In this he says: "When we see a great work of the creative imagination, a striking picture or a powerful drama, what is the essence of the fascination it exercises over us? Is it not because we find concentrated into a brief statement . . . or a few symbols . . . a wide range of human emotions and feelings which we, in the long course of experience, have been consciously or unconsciously classifying?" In short, the artist, through his intuitive processes, has made the same kind of summation which the scientist makes from his patient collection of measurable facts.

Monday . . . April 26

Victor Schwab, of Schwab & Beatty, whose work I have always admired, sends me a copy of his little book, "How to Write a Good Advertisement." In this he, too, makes some points recently noted here

148

about the intuitive processes. Of course, what I would be glad to trade him a couple of eyeteeth for are his records of pull on mail order ads.

Tuesday . . . April 27

Hoist by my own petard! A client wanted an ad to promote the Red Cross appeal for blood donors. Working on it overcame my own procrastination on this most real of all civilian opportunities, so up and did it. The procedure is magnificently simple, painless, efficient, and human. And it leaves you with the positive knowledge that you have saved at least one life.

Wednesday . . . April 28

The New York *Times* has been carrying some interesting reports on a recent outbreak among the jitterbugs there. One neurologist whom they interviewed about it said: "All of life, all humanity, the cosmos itself, is built upon the beat principle . . . One of the secrets of Hitler's power as an orator is in his reiteration, in the beat, the pulse, the rhythm of his speech." Here is stated what every powerful copywriter knows. It is this beat in copy which is so often damaged when the literal minded begin to edit it.

Thursday . . . April 29

Talked with a member of the economic staff of the Coordinator of Inter-American Affairs. He fears,

149

and says the South Americans fear, an overenthusi-
astic commercial invasion of those countries by us
in the post-war period. If we descend upon them
with the appetites of a swarm of locusts we shall
be resisted. But if we come prepared to plant, to
till, to harvest, and to share with them in the steady
development of their countries we will be wel-
comed.

Friday . . . April 30

A sailor boy, with the insignia of a Navy photog-
rapher on his sleeve, showed up in the office this
morning. He had managed to wangle a day's leave
to see if he could peddle some pictures of his own
made in off hours, and he had traveled all night at
his own expense to do it. When I took him to our
art department he saw a current exhibit of water
colors there, and fell on it with the eager little animal sounds of a starving man. Here is one boy, at
least, who is living in the hope of something better
than war.

May, 1943

Saturday . . . May 1

Woke at the farm this morning to find a new chestnut filly, out of the old Morgan mare, wabbling around the corral. A creature as gentle as a kitten, and already showing signs of that instinctive liking for men which always distinguished her mother. I promptly named her May Day.

Sunday . . . May 2

ON THE NATURE OF ADVERTISING KNOWLEDGE. Recently I sat on a committee with five other experienced advertising men, to plan a war publicity program. I was struck by the speed with which we harmonized our thinking. The basis for this was a common training in getting at the heart of a problem, and a common sensitivity to the pulse beats of public opinion. It is the process of cultivating this sensitivity which is the most important element in advertising education now. Years of work with our material is, of course, the great contributing factor. But unless the mental pores are kept open in certain ways it seems that this material has very little effect.

151

Monday . . . May 3

After years of resisting the temptation, I finally fell today for one of the finest of the minima cameras, with a fast *f.1.9 lens.* I began making pictures as a boy, with the first Brownie which Eastman ever put out. It cost $2—a whole week's pay. Photography has taken a goodly sum of money from me since, but I consider it one of the best investments I have made. It taught me to see pictures; and it taught me something of the preciseness which is required whenever the hands must be trained to do good work. In a world made up of so much loose talk, as advertising is, this is something.

Tuesday . . . May 4

At lunch I listened to the editor of a well-known magazine expound the beliefs behind his editing. Apparently his chief guide to the selection of material is a continuing reading rating of editorial contents. This appears to me to be two dimensional editing—length and breadth, with no depth. The *Reader's Digest* was a successful magazine when it was only a convenient digest. It became a great magazine when it began to publish articles of its own, designed to influence a course of action. An editor who is after popularity alone will end up by winning just that.

Wednesday . . . May 5

A correspondent, who identifies himself (?) only

152

as an agency employe, berates me for my recent entry about labor unions. He does not see how I can possibly be a sincere believer in unions and at the same time be speculating on methods for destroying them. Here is the gap between the partisan and the professional. The problems and techniques of the publicist may, in my view, be studied quite apart from the ends for which they are used. Just as an army staff may train itself in devising plans for the invasion of a friendly country, so I like to exercise on hypothetical problems which might be presented to a manipulator of public opinion.

Thursday . . . May 6

When I first came into the advertising business one of the giants of those days was John Lee Mahin. His name was known from coast to coast, wherever advertising men gathered. Then the day came when, standing by the doorway into an advertising convention, I saw Mr. Mahin ask for admission without a soul there but me recognizing his name. As the Bible story says: "A new King arose in the land who knew not Joseph." That new king, in the form of a new generation, is always coming on; and all Big Shots are hereby respectfully reminded of their fate.

Friday . . . May 7

Having a car which I need to move permanently from one state to another, I went today to my local rationing board to see if an extra gas allowance for this purpose could be secured. Either this board's staff is badly overworked, or it is hopelessly organized. There was no provision for the orderly handling of inquirers, and it took me about an hour merely to get an application blank. The man next to me said, with wrath, that his application had been filed for two months, with no action, and now appeared to be lost. Meantime, several pompous gents, with all the earmarks of politicos, strolled in and out in a knowledgeable way. Later, by locating one of these, I was assured that my application would receive prompt attention.

Saturday . . . May 8

Another unseasonable day, raw and cold. Even the deep-rooted alfalfa seems to be standing still, and I am afraid that we will be at least two weeks late in the first cutting this year. With alfalfa prices the highest I have ever seen in our neighborhood that's a loss which can be calculated in substantial terms. The weather man may be a joke in the city, but to a farmer he takes on the character of an industrial engineer.

Sunday . . . May 9

ON THE NATURE OF ADVERTISING KNOWLEDGE. The great discovery of American production genius was what could be accomplished when big problems are broken down into little

154

ones. This made the miracle of the assembly lines possible. A man begins to get somewhere in the accumulation of advertising knowledge when he adopts the same principle. Let him tackle this big subject in little bits and it becomes manageable. Why, for instance, do we start an ad with a headline? How do we *know* that such a practice increases advertising effectiveness? Let him answer that one first, and then move on.

Monday . . . May 10

Standing in line to buy a railroad ticket, I was reminded of the old saying that there is very little wrong with a business that orders won't cure. For years the railroads were in the financial and economic doldrums, and many were the grandiose schemes devised to save them. But now the movement of men and goods for war, the shortages in ship, automobile, and air transportation, and the greater prosperity of millions, are taxing all rail facilities. Result: debts being paid off, bankruptcies being voided, and rail stocks being bid up. Even John Lewis and the coal operators could probably resolve their problems if they had enough orders to operate mines at capacity.

Tuesday . . . May 11

Lunched with an executive of one of our big department stores. He said the demand for merchandise continued to be insatiable, and that so far they had been able to keep supply somewhere near it only by all sorts of buying ingenuity. In many out-of-the-way spots they have discovered little, unknown producers of unique articles, whose output in total has helped substantially in the maintenance of the store's volume.

Wednesday . . . May 12

The Art of Advertising is concerned with selling goods, whereas the Art of the Advertising Business is concerned with selling advertisers. The distinction is important, especially for the beginner, who must in the end learn both trades. To learn the Art of Advertising, which is the solid foundation, take your eyes off the big color pages, and pay close attention to the little ads in newspapers and magazines—to the medical "readers," the mail order gadgets, and the food specialties. Pay particular attention to the ads which are repeated again and again; these are known pullers. Study them closely to see how they get that itch for orders into them.

Thursday . . . May 13

One subject which has been highlighted by the war is the question of small business vs. big in this country. We are beginning to realize that there may be some basic differences, of great social importance, between them. One is in the nature of the business ownership. A proprietor who is operating on and risking his own capital is what we really

156

think of when we talk about "free enterprise." It is not so clear that the management of a big corporation, which has very little personal ownership in it, is in the same position, and is entitled to the same degree of freedom.

Friday . . . May 14

Years ago Professor Judd of the University of Chicago showed how the consumption of reading matter began to rise in this country after the introduction of the McGuffey Readers taught the oncoming generations how to read. I thought of this today after listening to a group of educators discuss developments in Visual Education—that is, teaching by films and other visual devices. Here is a movement which might have equally far-reaching effects —on literature and on advertising.

Saturday . . . May 15

Went down to southern Ohio, to my family home, and found the dogwood, redbud, and lilacs in late bloom. There is no fairer land than this one, with its gentle hills, rolling farms, and quiet villages. The Revolutionary soldiers of the Order of the Cincinnati thought so, too, when they came to settle these parts in the days of America's youth. They left upon the land the imprints of a society of free men which even modern industrialism has not yet wiped out.

Sunday . . . May 16

Spent much of the day reading a new life of John Morgan, the brilliant Confederate raider who taught the military world new tactics in the use of cavalry. In July, 1862, he escaped from a trap of Federal troops by capturing the town of Cynthiana, Ky., where my mother was a girl of five. On the morning after the battle she was taken to Morgan's camp by my grandfather, a southern supporter. There they found the Colonel just beginning his retreat south. Though in the heart of enemy-held country, this dashing commander swung the little girl to the saddle before him, and gaily rode her home before departing. And if you don't believe it, says my mother, you can see the very horse, with him upon it, in the Lexington, Ky., statue to this day. A Rebel still, and proud of it.

Monday . . . May 17

There are many ways to start an ad, but one of the best, if not *the* best, is to tell the reader how to get something he already wants. The formula is simple enough, but the real problem is to put your finger on that want. It may be something so obvious—like the merchandise itself—that you will tend to overlook it, and start farther back than you need to. Or it may be something so obscure—like pieces of the Blarney stone—that it takes sharp eyes to find it. But I note that all the really successful ad writers spend more time studying people's wants than anything else.

Tuesday . . . May 18

Riding a crowded streamliner today, in which every space was filled, and people sat up overnight in the club car, I thought that the great unsung heroes of our civilization are the Pullman porters. For many years I spent as much as one-third of all my nights in their care, and if there is any finer body of public servants anywhere than these men I can't think who it may be. Inasmuch as historians commonly neglect to record such really significant features of a day, I would like to see a statue of a Pullman porter erected, say in the nation's capital. Maybe *Advertising Age* could start a fund for one. I'll chip in if the Pullman Company will.

Wednesday . . . May 19

Went to see an experiment in Occupational Therapy being conducted for convalescing soldiers, by one of our military hospitals. The boys were as busy as the traditional beavers, making things with their hands—carving linoleum prints, modeling animals in clay, and making useful articles for themselves out of scrap leather. The teachers were all volunteer handicraftsmen, and both they and the pupils were having a hearty time. I have seen lots of tangled-up ad men get over the jitters with a day of just such work, and it looked to me as though these tough *hombres* were getting the same kind of results.

Thursday . . . May 20

A friend of mine on the Yale faculty sends me a pamphlet in which he and a colleague propose a complete revamping of the educational methods in law schools. In it he stresses the fact that lawyers have become the most influential policy-making people of our time, in government and in business. They have certainly crept up on us in the advertising business in the last few years; and from what I have seen them do to make selling ineffective I am ready to vote that they need some kind of change in their education.

Friday . . . May 21

A mail order client came in today with a letter he had received from a woman, in answer to a circular one which I had written for him recently. She said his letter had appealed to her deepest emotions, and made her want to know him better. Was he married, and could he send her a photograph of himself? Now the client wants me to answer her so as to keep the customer and lose the admirer. What a business!

Saturday . . . May 22

For three months my Airedale has been lost, but today I found him. The people who picked him up

160

on the roadside had treated him well. But when he saw me, he grabbed my hand in his mouth, and raced me up and down their yard in a frenzy of joy. Tonight he is sleeping again outside my door, and I can hear that friendly thump of his tail on the floor whenever he hears me move.

Sunday . . . May 23

Another rainy Sunday, just right for a log fire and a new book. So picked up Dr. Fosdick's last one, "On Being a Real Person." Almost anybody could get something for himself out of this, but an advertising man can get a lot if he reads it as the case book of a man who probably has seen the insides of as many people as anybody living.

Monday . . . May 24

Most ad men long for a product of their own on which they can exercise their talents. If they can make money for others (they think) why not for themselves? And besides, there is the longing to produce advertising which will require no other okay than their own. Many have tried it, and some, like the late A. W. Erickson, have made marked successes; but more have failed. I failed the first two times I tried it, but hit on the third and fourth. But whether it brings success or failure, the experience is highly educational. The man who has wrestled with the total problems of a business, and spent his own money for advertising space or time, has more respect for his employer or client, and is a better, more mature advertising man and counselor.

Tuesday . . . May 25

It has always been easy for me to be *sympatico* with our Spanish American neighbors. My father was born in the north of Ireland, in County Tyrone, where, as he used to say, "the face of an honest man never was known." I went there once to climb the family tree. The roots, I found, were Scotch Presbyterian; but a shipwrecked Spanish sailor had gotten into our branch at some time, and left traces of his name and temperament. I was, myself, christened with a Spanish form of a Scotch name, although I have never used it. However, I have carried on the tradition by naming my Scotch terrier Chico McGillicuddy. He sometimes looks a little dour at such levity.

Wednesday . . . May 26

Jim O'Shaughnessy sends me a piece he has written, proposing that advertising men be given a place at the Peace Table, when it comes. I wish I might believe there are some among us with the stature for such recognition, but I am afraid the facts of life are agin it. We are too shallow rooted a profession, and do not have enough of what Vincent Sheean calls "a sense of history." But we are young yet; give us time.

162

Thursday . . . May 27

Churchill and Roosevelt are certainly the greatest team of politicians, statesmen, and world leaders of today. They carry responsibilities which one might think would bow them down. Yet I never see a photograph of either of them which does not reveal that comfortable look which comes only to a man in whose line business is very, very good.

Friday . . . May 28

Had a letter from a man who has been flirting with me for years about doing some advertising for him. But I know several people who have tried and never succeeded in writing copy to please him. Because he keeps waiting for the perfect copy, the perfect medium, and the perfect set of conditions, he never gets his advertising started. Secretary Chase said: "The way to resume (specie payments) is to resume." And the way to begin advertising is to begin.

Saturday . . . May 29

Poetry is not my dish, and I seldom develop a taste for it. But here is a verse, found on an old English ale mug, which so exactly describes my condition and sentiments that I wish I might have had the wit to write it:

163

Let the wealthy and great
Roll in splendour and state
I envy them not I declare It
    I eat my own lamb
My own chickens and ham
I shear my own fleece and I wear it
I have lawns I have bowers
I have fruits I have flowers
The lark is my morning alarmer
    So my jolly boys now
Here's God speed the plough
Long life and success to the farmer

Sunday . . . May 30

Here endeth the fifty-second week of the keeping of this Diary. It has been fun for me to do, has seemed to please some readers, and has certainly irritated others. Sometimes, as I read it over, I sound more critical and cynical than I have meant to be. I shall have to reform, and dispense more of that treacle to which the readers of business papers are accustomed.

Monday . . May 31

Studying what people want, and telling them ways to get it, are the ad man's business. In Dr. Fosdick's recent book he says: "Of the three major figures in modern psychiatry, Freud may roughly be represented as saying that man wants most of all to be loved; Jung as saying that he wants most of all to feel secure; Adler that he wants most of all

164

to feel significant." Love, security, and significance sometimes flow together, and are all yields of the same situation. But at times the yearning for one will take such priority as to sacrifice the other two. Remember the flagpole sitters?

June, 1943

Talked today with a man who is always eager to discuss some large, general scheme for human welfare. Yet in all his personal relationships he is one of the most selfish men I have ever known; and I have observed over the years that he never weeds his own garden. What is this strange paradox in the humanitarian's character? Communism, which glorifies the proletariat, has produced some monsters of human cruelty. And I note that New Dealers, with all their love of the Common Man, display more venom toward those who disagree with them than do Democrats or Republicans.

Started making myself a file on ways in which advertising has worked. All of us carry a series of such cases around in our heads, but I have long wanted to get mine down on paper and in orderly form. Took as my No. 1 case a company for which advertising does the complete selling job, getting cash orders at a profit direct from the printed page. My hope is to secure enough cases in each such classification to lead to some general conclusions about the conditions under which advertising may be expected to perform in certain ways. Neil Borden made the first careful approach of this kind to advertising knowledge, and a good one, in his case book for the Harvard business school.

Thursday . . . June 3

For more years than she would like to have me tell, my wife has been getting her "vittles" from the advertising business. But she has always contended that it couldn't last, and that I ought to get into something "real." A year ago she felt sure that, at last, this war was going to prove her right, and I am afraid that the revival in advertising volume is a great disappointment to her. It is hard for lots of people to understand that the power of persuasion is a commodity that will always be marketable.

Friday . . . June 4

By and large, we get pretty well paid in this advertising business. In fact, our salary scale for talent seems excessive to most manufacturers. Yet, I am constantly surprised by the number of men among us who are eternally hard up. Apparently capacity to save has nothing to do with capacity to earn. A fellow who told me that he "couldn't save a nickel" when he was getting $5,000 a year, still tells me he can't on $30,000.

Saturday . . . June 5

Picked my first sour pie cherries, and declared the summer season officially open, calendar or no calendar. Brought them to the cook with a jar of my finest leaf lard, rendered from last fall's hogs, and saved just for shortening pie crusts. Sometimes it seems to me that Nature herself conspires against my waistline.

Sunday . . . June 6

Opened the last can of a pipe tobacco which I have been getting from England for many years. It came from a little shop on Pall Mall, just off St. James' Street. Having customers for it all over the world, they had learned how to pack an export tin so that the tobacco kept moist and fresh in any climate indefinitely. I hear that the shop has been bombed out of existence. But I am betting that my next shipment will arrive on schedule, because when it comes to export England "delivers the goods." If we think they are going to let us take any foreign markets away from them without a struggle we can guess again.

Monday . . . June 7

A correspondent suggests that I devote some space in this Diary to criticism of current advertisements. I take it that he means criticism in its real sense of critical examination, leading either to praise or blame. But that comes under the heading of dan-

gerous sports. I have never, myself, submitted an
ad for one of the established advertising awards—
holding it to be doubtful whether any outsider can
ever evaluate an advertisement when he doesn't
know all that it was designed to do, or the limitations under which it had to do it.

Tuesday . . . June 8

Visited a small town, in an area where there are
no war industries. Talked with the one banker and
several of the retail merchants. They all told me
that more money was flowing into the town than
ever before in its history, being sent there by service men and by those who have gone off to work
in war industries. This money is giving the retail
merchants the best business they ever had, in spite
of consumer goods shortages. Even the deadest of
inventory items is moving. Thus does economics
often confound its prophets.

Wednesday . . . June 9

I am, I think, a shy man; and particularly am I
tongue-tied in the presence of strange ladies. So
while I am flattered when a woman reader of this
Diary writes me that she enjoys it, I am a little taken
aback when she personalizes her admiration. Or
am I?

Thursday . . . June 10

The volume of advertising rolled up for the last
war bond drive is impressive evidence of the suc-

cess of the War Advertising Council in "marshalling the forces," as it set out to do. But the percentage of total bond sales made to individuals, while better than that of the preceding drive, is still not good enough to be very good testimony for the effectiveness of this advertising. Why did it not accomplish more? First, perhaps, because the effort is still not as well coordinated as it might be. And second, because the volume of sales effort did not match the advertising volume. At least, in my own case nobody ever actually asked me to buy a bond, and few people whom I know were personally solicited for an order.

Friday . . . June 11

It looks to me as though we had made a good deal of progress toward the socialist ideal of the classless state. We are now down to just about two classes: government inspectors and those inspected. The only potential political candidate who seems to see any issue in that fact is Governor Bricker of Ohio.

Saturday . . . June 12

Some days life on a farm is just O.D.T.A.A. This morning I woke to find a swarm of winged ants on my bedroom ceiling. Apparently they had nested in the roof during the winter, and had just decided to move. No sooner had the spray gun blitzed these than there came a report of new gopher damage in the orchard. When the traps for these gentry were set the water pump was out of order. Then, to top off this perfect country day, came a hired man who wanted to quit for higher wages in a war plant. Don't buy a farm unless you have first learned the meaning of the verb "to cope."

Sunday . . . June 13

Had a letter from a friend of mine who has spent most of his life as a political reformer. As such, he was tireless in his attacks on the chicanery of politicians. Then, under Roosevelt, he was given a job as an important administrator, and little by little I have watched him become a practicing politician, indulging in much of the finagling which he formerly attacked. It is unfortunate but true that there is no complete defense of either politics or advertising which does not involve some indictment of human nature.

Monday . . . June 14

In the old days an advertising agent could count on a good many perquisites from publishers—sets of books, boxes of oranges, and whatnot at Christmas. But as the business became more aseptic this custom, unhappily, fell into disfavor. I am reminded of it by the receipt of a very handsome, and very much appreciated, book of dog stories from a reader of this Diary; and by the gift of three pamphlets of homespun philosophy which another has published. Such generosity should be encouraged! Anybody got any meat stamps to spare?

Tuesday . . . June 15

A client of mine has begun to supply all his employes with a daily dose of vitamin tablets—a respectable item of increased cost of doing business. If ever there was an illustration of the power of pure faith this vitamin business is it. While there is plenty of scientific evidence of specific results from vitamin intake, few normal individuals ever see it in their own experience. Probably this client will never see it, either, in traceable increased productiveness or decreased absenteeism. But he "believes" it is a "good thing." However, about 15% of his employes apparently "believe" he is only trying to "speed them up," so they will have none of it.

Wednesday . . . June 16

Finished reading a book on land resources, put out by three men at one of our state universities. It is an excellent scientific report, but because the subject involves hot political and racial conflicts in that particular state, I could see all through it where the authors had pulled their punches. Our state universities have become great institutions, and many of them do as fine research in pure science as is being done. But it is doubtful whether there will ever be in them, or in any government institution, as complete academic freedom as the endowed universities provide. Here is one of the dangers in a taxation policy which destroys at its source the great accumulations of private wealth.

172

Thursday . . . June 17

We are, I believe, the country which spends on education more per capita than any other in the world. We certainly buy the most books and reading matter of every kind. And yet we have an odd sort of reluctance to admit our belief in learning. So we invented such phrases as "high brow" and "five dollar words" to cry down any pretensions to intellectual activity; and most of us go about very carefully guarding ourselves against any such damaging charge.

Friday . . . June 18

Post-war planning may be getting to be a subject like Mark Twain's weather. It is easy to talk about it and hard to do anything about it, especially in the field of marketing. It is also easy to feel that something has been done about it when a vice-president or a committee in charge of post-war planning has been appointed. In trying to come to grips with the subject in my business I have found I could get some help from "Markets After the War," issued by the Department of Commerce.

Saturday . . . June 19

Visited with a country neighbor, a lorn widow, who runs the exchange for our rural telephone line. She gets a house and $40 a month for her job, so statistically she is among the under-privileged. But her wants are simple, and by frugal management

173

she keeps well and happy on this income. And with her radio, the *Reader's Digest*, and all those telephone conversations, I find that she always has more to tell me than I her.

Sunday . . . June 20

Running over my library, I was reminded of a day, many years ago, when a solicitor on the old *Christian Herald*, Arthur Acheson, astonished me by the presentation of a book he had written, called "Dark Lady of the Sonnets." I then discovered that, in his spare time, he had made himself one of the leading Shakespearean scholars of the day—a fact which was recognized when George Bernard Shaw quoted him in one of his prefaces. But this scholarly pursuit only increased Arthur's humanness. Calling one day on a tough advertiser in my bailiwick, he was told: "Hell, I wouldn't use your paper: your people are too religious." To which Arthur succinctly replied: "Listen, mister, we're not so G—d—d religious!"

Monday . . . June 21

Fifteen years ago Elmer Davis of OWI fame wrote a novel about King David, called "The Giant Killer." In it he showed the Psalmist as a man who always got the credit for other men's deeds—including the killing of Goliath—and always escaped the blame for his own misdeeds and mistakes. Wonder whether Elmer ever sees a parallel as he surveys the Washington scene today?

174

Tuesday . . . June 22

I have a friend who used to say that his favorite reading was a book called "Who's Who, What's He Got, and How to Get It" by Dun and Bradstreet. He would need a revised edition today. The surplus buying power now spread throughout the land is like an unworked placer mine. Anybody who wants to get rich need only solve the problem of devising something to sell, like a new religion, which requires no manufacturing facilities.

Wednesday . . . June 23

The publications are getting tougher about observance of their closing dates, and rightly so. There is no real excuse for nine out of ten requests for extensions. In most cases the root of the trouble is the failure to hold copy people to their advance deadlines. Because writers dawdle past their dates, waiting for inspiration and mood, everybody else who is to work on the job gets squeezed. It is nonsense to say that you can't "get an idea" by 4 o'clock on Tuesday, and every experienced writer knows it.

Thursday . . . June 24

Received from the president of a leading corporation an elaborate booklet, extolling in words and pictures what his company is doing to win the war. I suppose this is at least the twenty-fifth brochure of this kind which has come into my hands, and I

175

must say that I am getting damned tired of them. Somehow or other big business always forgets the lady who did protest too much.

Friday . . . June 25

Rubbed my eyes and read again this bit in a government pamphlet on post-war planning: "A peacetime level of production which approaches the capacity of available manpower after the war means a substantial increase over prewar standards of living. To reach this higher standard of living, consumers must be persuaded to buy more things than they have ever had before . . . This calls for better market analysis, more sales research, more imagination and ingenuity in developing new products or new markets for old ones, more strenuous efforts to improve promotion and distribution methods." Who let this wolf into the New Deal sheepfold?

Saturday . . . June 26

Not being a Catholic (with a capital C, but I hope with a lower case one), I have never had occasion to know any of the black-robed Sisters of that faith. Indeed, I was raised to think of them as completely withdrawn from this world. But recently, having established a hat-tipping acquaintance with some Sisters of St. Francis who run a school in our neighborhood, I thought to learn more about them. So my wife and I invited four of them to lunch today, and they graciously accepted. Remembering St.

Paul's injunction we took a little wine for the stomach's sake, and had as jolly, fluent, and human a meal as I ever sat to. Thus is another childish notion outgrown.

Sunday . . . June 27

One of my country neighbors, a hard-working, honest man, is constantly bedeviled by emergencies. The business of farming, by its very nature, has a higher percentage of these than does city manufacturing, but this man has more than his share. I used to think him a child of misfortune, but now I can see that he creates most of his troubles by a plain lack of foresight. This seems to be one of the qualities in which men born free are not born equal.

Monday . . . June 28

Spent the day in a small town which is the capital of a state. Having some business there which brought me into contact with different groups of citizens, I soon discovered which families formed the socially elite. No town, however small, is without such a group; but how it forms itself no man can tell. In this town neither the richest family nor the leading official one is counted within the magic circle. For the most part those without this circle do not care too much, but sometimes they feel a sense of bafflement at the intangible barriers which keep them there.

177

Tuesday . . . June 29

As I go about the country, talking with a good many kinds of people, I find that the subject matter for conversation does not vary much, percentage-wise. First, and properly so, comes the weather—sure instinct for the importance of our physical environment. Then comes man, quite literally embracing woman, with all the ramifications thereof. Most of the rest can be summarized under food and drink, business and war. Beyond this I am reminded of what William James' carpenter said—that there is not much difference between one man and another, but what little there is, is important.

Wednesday . . . June 30

I hear that a big radio contract which was recently let involved a speculative competition among three agencies. It is said that considerable money was spent by them in auditioning programs—probably in total more than any net profit the contract can yield. Excess profit taxes being what they are, this does not mean much today, even to the losers. But the practice remains a bad one, not only for the waste it injects into agency operations as a whole, but because it is essentially an unsound procedure for the advertiser. The wiser ones no longer encourage it.

178

July, 1943

Thursday . . . July 1

Speaking of "a sense of history," I wonder that more of us do not have it about our own trade. I find few advertising men who have ever heard of, much less read, George P. Rowell's "Forty Years an Advertising Agent." Yet here are exhibited the social forces which made modern publishing and advertising, in the years between 1860 and 1900. The most up-to-date Yale-Man-in-Advertising might be amazed at how much he rediscovers of what Rowell knew then.

Friday . . . July 2

(From a letter to a young writer.) You say the man went down the street. But *how* did he go? Did he walk, run, amble, sidle, limp, hurry, saunter, caper, trip, jog, stumble, stagger, swing, rush, dash, etc.? With one verb you can make me see the mood as well as the action of that man—providing, of course, that you first saw him accurately yourself.

Saturday . . . July 3

Instead of the lark it is, in fact, a humming bird

179

who is my morning alarmer at this season of the year. When the sunrise comes over the mountain, without benefit of Kate Smith, it strikes the hollyhocks growing by my bedroom window. Almost at once the humming bird is hovering over their blossoms, and his wings are whirring me a warning that it is time to be up and doing.

Sunday . . . July 4

There is a creek flowing through my farm which is one of the Little Waters which goes to make up a mighty and famous river. When the spring runoff or a cloudburst comes, my creek contributes its part to soil erosion, silting, and floods. Then we all begin to talk about the Government "doing something" to control the mighty river. But if I and all my neighbors were doing all we might, by better husbandry, to control the Little Waters, the Big Waters would be no problem. Maybe in the same way we overlook the Little Waters of politics and business—in the wards and precincts above whose level politics cannot rise; and in the enterprise of small businesses which must catch the trickles that make our mighty corporations and our whole economic system.

Monday . . . July 5

Received today my first V-Mail letter, written somewhere in the Pacific, by Arthur Hallam, an advertising man now in the Navy. He says: "Your item of March 7 interested me very much because for years I have been trying to promote a system of examinations for advertising men. . . . The Four A's should be the one to initiate the program. . . . Ability to pass examinations is not a final criterion, but it would at least offer some sort of standard to the advertiser that he does not have now. . . . When we get back to the States I am going to get in touch with you again on this." Fighting for a better world and thinking about how to do something in his part of it, too.

Tuesday . . . July 6

The real pay-off to the keeping of this Diary comes in such mail as it brings me. I feel as though I had made a new friend when I hear from J. H. Mitchell, the Minneapolis advertising agent, that we have shared some experiences. And when Fred Hauck of the Columbus Better Business Bureau tells me that some ideas expressed here have helped him, and sends me some that help me. I even get a kick out of the Cleveland gentleman who thinks that most of what I put down, especially that about the New Deal, is helping to make up the fertilizer shortage.

Wednesday . . . July 7

Some marriages are reminders of the fact that everybody can sell somebody. But we are not as often reminded of the opposite fact that nobody can sell everybody. Most people and propositions have

181

their natural limitations. These are inherent in personality and temperament if in nothing else. Advertising which keys a proposition to a certain kind of person may be highly successful as long as it stays true to type. When it tries to be all things to all men it endangers the personality it has established and makes an appeal to nobody.

Thursday . . . July 8

Marvelous new *things* are being projected for us in the post-war world. I don't doubt that we shall have them, and value them. But if all we are going to get out of this war is the same kind of gadget development that we got out of the last one, then we shall have another unhappy ending sooner or later. Man still does not live by better ice boxes alone. We need the inventors and salesmen of new ideas of social equilibrium as well.

Friday . . . July 9

If any man has a taste for making type talk he will want to own a copy of "Paragraphs on Printing" by that Old Master among book designers, Bruce Rogers. Such a book is the next best thing to standing alongside such a workman day after day, and catching the secrets of his skill. Even more, it is the revelation of what a good life there is in the honest adherence to a trade. It makes me homesick for the boy who started out in life to be a designer of books, and switched to advertising them instead.

182

Saturday . . . July 10

Picked my Stella apricots, and set the women to canning some and drying others. I like to work among the graceful branches and fresh green leaves of this tree, and I like the delicate coloring as well as the taste of the just-ripe fruit. When my wife filled a black Indian bowl with some of the choicest ones I felt it was a dish to set before a king.

Sunday . . . July 11

Sat this evening with a group of neighbors, men and women, smoking and talking of this and that. The cigaret brands present were Camels, Chesterfields, Old Golds, Philip Morris, and Tareytons. Somebody mentioned the *Reader's Digest* article on cigaret advertising, and it developed that nearly everybody had read it. The Ad Man got a little friendly joshing about it, and then everybody went on to something else, each puffing his favorite brand.

Monday . . . July 12

A correspondent asks for my definition of the objective of advertising. That's like asking for the objective of electricity. I doubt if one can be written which is broad enough to cover all cases, and specific enough to be useful. The important thing is to have no astigmatism about the objective in any particular case. Until you can say exactly what you

want the reader to do, think, feel, or believe, you
are not ready to devise how to get it done. And,
incidentally, an agreement on this in advance will
harmonize a lot of copy critics.

Tuesday . . . July 13

Nowadays we tend to discount the value of what
used to be almost the sole objective of advertising;
namely, to create familiarity. That familiarity alone
is a great sales asset, and that it can be secured
most quickly through advertising repetition, was almost the earliest discovery about advertising. Thus
all the early salesmen of space preached such doc-
trines as "Keep Your Name Before the Public,"
"Repetition Makes Reputation," "Keeping Everlast-
ingly At It Brings Success." If we hadn't forgotten
how true this is there would be more consistent
schedules in publications.

Wednesday . . . July 14

My impression is somewhat different from that
of Westbrook Pegler. I think, on the whole, the war
has given advertising writers a thrill. Many of the
generation which just escaped the draft never really
liked to sell merchandise, never had the old-timer's
itch for orders. The chance to devote their writing
talents to the selling of ideas instead of goods, and
to feel that they might be making a war contribution in doing so, has been a great relief to them. As
witness the ease with which the War Advertising
Council gets volunteers.

184

Thursday . . . July 15

Advertising couldn't live except under a division-of-labor economy, with a high degree of specialization. (And vice versa.) Nevertheless, if I had the ordering of the universe I would require every soul to supply some of its basic wants directly—that is, to raise some of its food, make some of its clothes, gather its own fuel, or something of the sort. There is no satisfaction comparable to it, and there is no road which leads so surely to psychic health. Those radishes you get out of your Victory garden may cost more than the grocer's, but they'll be worth it.

Friday . . . July 16

The hardest job I have is to lure ad writers out of ivory towers. The flight from reality is instinctive in most of us writing coves. We think we have solved a problem when we have given a neat expression to it; and the intractability of material, human or inanimate, bores us. We know that ditch water is full of interesting zoological specimens but how we do hate to dredge it.

Saturday . . . July 17

Years ago H. L. Mencken observed that one popular American delusion is that all male Negroes have fine tenor voices. Another is that all black dirt is rich in plant food and will grow anything. A gentleman who wanted to sell me a truck load of it to-

185

day was disconcerted when I ran a sample through my soil testing kit, and found it slightly deficient in nitrogen and extremely deficient in phosphate.

Sunday . . . July 18

If you want to know one thing that people are really interested in, take their pictures and listen to their comments on the prints. They'll never notice your perfect composition, skillful cropping, or technical excellence. The sole question is how do *they* look. Like the bride and groom standing in front of Niagara Falls. Or an advertiser scanning the size of the package.

Monday . . . July 19

Studied some records of a split-run copy test which were said to indicate that pictures of the product in use were far better than any human interest ones. In this one case the record did indeed indicate this; but no scientist would deduce a summer from one such swallow. Too hasty generalizations from very limited evidence are still the curse of too many of our copy researchers.

Tuesday . . . July 20

Amazed to find myself listed as an "Economist" in the new directory of a club to which I have been admitted. I wish I could believe that this meant a recognition of the actual and important part which

186

advertising plays in economics, but I am afraid it is just another bit of genteelism and intellectual snobbishness. I can see the serious-faced committee who compiled the directory puzzling how to list me without letting that terrible word "advertising" tag along.

Wednesday . . . July 21

Years ago there was a distinguished economist at the University of California who held that his profession would never really get anywhere until it had blended with it that of the social psychologist. That always appeared to me to be profoundly true. In a work-a-day way the advertising man may represent a foreshadowing of that blend. If the rise of doctors and surgeons can be traced up a barber's pole, to what heights may we not yet climb?

Thursday . . . July 22

If there is any blame to be placed for the confusion in Washington, says my old neighbor Harold Ickes, it should be on the business men there. Speaking from some experience in that quarter, I would say that the business men who were called in have made only one major mistake, namely, being willing to accept great responsibilities without adequate authority to deliver on them. Some have done this because they were promised the authority and then found the promise not kept; some because they were then too patriotic to leave in the midst of an

187

emergency; some because the light that beats about the throne, once enjoyed, is hard to withdraw from. Chester Davis is the only one who had the courage to show up the situation exactly as it is; and, the resulting attempt to besmirch him was a most unbecoming performance.

Friday . . . July 23

Today I heard a tot of four ask its mother for a Kleenex on which to blow its nose. Think of the brand good-will and business asset inherent in such an incident! Patents come and patents go, but the statistical probability that this child and millions like him will go on following their established habits is where the real future of any business lies.

Saturday . . . July 24

A friend who has been down to Mexico on a business trip brought me back a pair of *tapaderos*. So, attaching them to my stirrups, the Palomino and I tried them out today in a three-hour ride. Part of the enjoyment in horseback riding is undoubtedly related to the heroic proportions one takes on, in one's own mind. *Tapaderos* increase this by giving a swagger to the outfit, and adding a touch of the dashing *caballero*.

Sunday . . . July 25

In a village near my farm there is a little dining place, run by a Frenchman and his wife, Charlie and

188

Mimi. Charlie was a sailor in the French Navy in the last war, and later a speak-easy operator in New York. Now he works by day in an essential material mine, to help beat the Germans again, and by night oversees his restaurant. When I dropped in this evening he was all wrought up over the merits of DeGaulle versus Giraud. What a rich and varied country this is!

Monday . . . July 26

Met a copywriter who used to work for me, and who has had six different jobs since. A lot of the boys and girls who write copy and make layouts these days seem to be getting into the habits of the old-time itinerant printers and barbers. They move from agency to agency at the clink of a coin, as if there were no such thing as building and growing with one firm, or loyalty to any vision beyond the week's pay envelope. Such people have a congenital employe psychology and, I have observed, seldom end up with a proprietary interest in anything.

Tuesday . . . July 27

Between the Federal Trade Commission and the *Reader's Digest* I am getting a bit confused. I don't quite know where harmless promotional coloration ends and misleading advertising begins. I note, for instance, that the owners of the *Digest* call themselves The Reader's Digest Association, Inc. Now that certainly suggests to me a cooperative, non-

189

profit, public service body, something like the National Geographic Society; but I understand that, in fact, it is a closely held family corporation, highly profitable to a few individuals. Again, because of its name and editorial presentation, most people seem to think the *Digest* is a sort of hit parade from all the best editorial minds. But I have been told that many of the articles it publishes are originated by the editors of the *Digest*, written to their order, and then "planted" in other lesser publications in order to maintain the digesting fiction. From my point of view, no less value is delivered to the readers by this kind of promotional coloration, but the FTC doesn't seem to hold with such hokum, so I don't know.

Wednesday . . . July 28

Spent the day in the field with a district salesman for a grocery specialty. These men, who have taken so many beatings from hard-boiled buyers, would be less than human if they did not enjoy their present position as allocators of stocks. But some of them are smart enough to foresee the day when they will again be supplicants for orders, and to go on building as much customer good will as they possibly can.

Thursday . . . July 29

Got into conversation with the man across from me in a railway diner, and found him to be a retired clothing manufacturer, with a Hebraic name.

190

Finding that we had a number of Jewish friends in common, it wasn't long before I began to hear of the fears of anti-Semitism which beset so many of these people today. Several times I have been approached on the subject of using publicity to combat this evil, but have never seen a way to make it effective. But it would be a good stroke of public relations if Jewish leaders could find some way to avoid association with other sources of irritation, such as in labor negotiations with Gentile manufacturers.

Friday . . . July 30

For my sins I have had to spend a good deal of time on trains again this week. Why the railway employes are not all quietly going mad is beyond me. The ticket sellers, in particular, seem to be caught in the intricacies of a procedure which is poorly designed to meet the demands now placed upon it. Surely some way could be found to package their product so they could get it off the shelf a lot quicker.

Saturday . . . July 31

It is good to go through the Middle West at this season of the year and see the fruits of the rich earth. In spite of the early floods, the fields of shocked wheat, the stands of corn, the orchards, and pastures, all give an effect of peace and plenty beyond our deserts in a war-torn world. Anybody looking for an America worth fighting for can see it here.

191

August, 1943

Sunday . . . August 1

Drove with my mother out to an Ohio farm, to buy some peaches she wanted for canning, and found the farmer busy running them through his grader. Being interested in fruit growing myself, I started in to see what I could learn about his varieties, cultural methods, and such. But somewhere in the conversation I mentioned cave storage, and that touched off the spring of romance in him. Caves of every kind were his secret passion, and when he once learned that I had visited the great Carlsbad Caverns he stopped the grader and wouldn't let me go until I had told him all I could remember of them. A starved man in the midst of plenty.

Monday . . . August 2

I see by the Washington correspondence in *Advertising Age* that there is an "authentic, but official" report that WPB plans certain things about paper allocations. Modifying authentic with official is something new, but sometimes it is hard to keep a typewriter from revealing the truth.

192

Tuesday . . . August 3

How much space does an ad really need for maximum effectiveness? As this decision does more to determine the cost of the advertising than anything else except copy, it seems to me that we give it too little attention. Our tendency is to let the publishers determine the answer by their more or less arbitrary divisions of space. I would like to see somebody really take this question apart, starting with the fact that for each ad there is some minimum space requirement, determined by length of copy, and then working through the other factors which must be considered—importance to be given the message, prestige of the advertiser, advertising competition, etc.

Wednesday . . . August 4

On the above question, I have made a few tests myself. I think I can demonstrate that, contrary to popular opinion, size of space itself has very little to do with securing optical attention. The eye of a stockholder in General Foods will apparently pick up a 2-inch, single column dividend notice about as quickly as it will a full page. But this doctrine will not be popular with publishers, so let it go.

Thursday . . . August 5

I note that the publishers of comics talk a good deal about the readability of their editorial technique. They also point out that it has a wide appeal to adults as well as children. And there is plenty of evidence from the reading-rating services to sustain them. But I also note that these publishers, in their own promotion matter, seldom use this technique. Maybe they don't think it carries conviction as well as it does entertainment—which is my own notion about it.

Friday . . . August 6

Came out to Chicago on the Century, and ran into several other ad men. One of them was telling me about a representative of his agency who recently left it, and took with him some business with which he had been entrusted. "Just a case of a kidnapper stealing the child," he said, "and the agency refusing to pay ransom." But the emphasis, I thought, ought to be on the "child," who has so trustingly gone off with a man who starts in business by betraying his employer.

Saturday . . . August 7

Our women folk constantly complain about the time we spend talking shop. But I doubt whether any woman understands that this is just one of the verbal signs of fraternalism which all animals make among their kind. At the root of it is the satisfaction we get out of being a member in good standing of our particular trade; of having the respect of our peers; and of trading experience with those who do not require a dictionary to understand us.

194

Sunday . . . August 8

A news-letter which I get from England says that the Russians are beginning to worry about American economic imperialism in the post-war world. I wouldn't have given it a thought if I had not recently talked with a woman who has made a fortune writing soap operas. She says the next big development in them is in the export field—that American advertisers will eventually take them around the world, just as American movie producers did Mickey Mouse. No wonder the Russians are worried!

Monday . . . August 9

Got into an elevator in the Graybar building, New York, to go up to the Four A's office. A little old man in a Western Union uniform was the only other passenger. As we started up, the operator turned to the messenger "boy" and said: "Monsieur, what is the leading wine of France?" To which the messenger replied: "C'est Burgundy." "C'est Burgundy?" questioned the operator. "Mais, oui," said the messenger, "c'est Burgundy!" Then both drew themselves up, clicked their heels, saluted, and said in unison: "Vive La France!" Sounds crazy, but that's the way it was.

Tuesday . . . August 10

A client of mine in the garment trade in a western city wanted to buy some Singer sewing machines, but no new ones were to be had. In his city he discovered 100 of just the kind he wanted, in storage since the wind-up of a local WPA project. But somebody in Washington had just ordered these crated and shipped to South America, and nothing could be done to divert them. Eventually the client discovered some more such machines in a second-hand dealer's in New York, which had come from a WPA project in Indianapolis. These were shipped west to him over the same miles that carried the other lot east, for shipment to South America. Viva La Planning!

Wednesday . . . August 11

Greatly pleased to receive today an invitation to participate in a post-war commerce symposium at one of Canada's great universities. There is a country and a people! Twenty-five years ago the little town of Perth, Ontario, used to be on my winter selling schedule, and I would stay there for several days at the Hicks House. In spite of deep snows and freezing temperatures, there was no heat to be had in the place except from a pot-bellied stove in the lounge and from the glasses in the bar. When I saw the Canadians there, taking their whisky neat in full tumblers, I used to think, as I do now, that they proved the reverse of James J. Hill's dictum: that the man on whom snow never falls isn't worth a damn.

196

Thursday . . . August 12

Some mail order advertising results suggest that there may be a space policy which might be called "the dangerous middle." I took a four-inch, single column ad which had long been successful as an inquiry producer in women's publications, and blew it up to a quarter page. The inquiry cost promptly went up. Then I took the same piece of copy, expanded it to include more selling material, and ran it in a full page, in color. The inquiry cost went down below that of the four-inch space.

Friday . . . August 13

Had a chance today to see the results of an incentive pay plan which a client of mine adopted three years ago. In that period his workers have nearly doubled their output and pay per man and woman. His total overhead costs have gone down about 25%, and his direct supervisory costs even more. He has lost few workers through the allurements of higher pay in other work, and these have been more than offset by the employes of competitors who have sought a place with him. The secret is that the wage rate originally established has never been lowered.

Saturday . . . August 14

A relative of mine has been employed in a civil service job for the War Department. Today he was called in by a superior and asked to sign his resignation. Congress, it was explained, had called for a reduction in the War Department's civil employes. Therefore my relative's unit was to be removed from the department's rolls and transferred bodily to another branch of government—where it would go right on with the same work at the same rates of pay. The Greeks had a word for it: hydra.

Sunday . . . August 15

Riding horseback along a back country road I saw a small land turtle crossing ahead of me. Just then a cottontail dashed out of the bushes on one side and into those on the other. So maybe I am the only living man who has actually seen the tortoise race the hare.

Monday . . . August 16

We are not yet making the progress we should in converting publication advertising to war. As I looked over the last issues of all the weeklies today I saw too many ads with nothing to sell, and nothing to say except "What a big boy am I!" With the shortage of manpower and paper which now exists, this begins to be a criminal waste of the communication facilities of this nation, and all of us concerned had better wake up to that fact.

Tuesday . . . August 17

Here is a nice little moral as well as business problem with which a friend of mine has been wres-

198

tling. His business is a small manufacturing one. His product is in good demand, but can hardly be classed as an essential one, even to civilian supply. So far he has been able to get materials and labor, so his business is not in distress. For over a year he has tried in every possible way to convert to war production, but because he is not in distress no government agency seems interested. There ought to be some way in which this efficient little working unit could add its bit to war manpower, without closing up shop and destroying a business which will be needed when postwar employment becomes a problem.

Wednesday . . . August 18

Heading for the far West, I ran into a bunch of radio people on their way to Hollywood. It seems to me that in this branch of our business there is more war consciousness, and more action about it, than in any other. Perhaps this is because our radio people are more showmen than salesmen—and the war is the biggest show on earth. Which is not to impugn their patriotism, either.

Thursday . . . August 19

Saw a well-known magazine publisher, at a western ranch resort, who had gone native in a big way —cowboy boots and pants, striped red shirt, and five-gallon Stetson. It seems that all most of us need is this kind of chance to release our too-suppressed instincts for colorful dress. But in an Indian village that I know, such visitors are summed up with the realistic comment: "Big hat; no cattle."

Friday . . . August 20

An old Indian friend of mine came to see me, and brought along his little drum, because he knows that I like to hear the songs of his people. After supper we sat around in the twilight while he tapped the drum and sang to it. One song came out which I hadn't heard before, and I asked what it was. "That song," he said, "from long time ago. Used to sing it to the women while they grind corn. Don't sing much any more; woman say: 'Go grocery —buy bread.'" Oh, Advertising!

Saturday . . . August 21

A new kind of war risk came home to me today. On a steep, winding, mountain road the hydraulic brakes of my son's car suddenly went haywire, and it ended up as a pile of junk in a ditch. Fortunately, the driver crawled out with only a broken shoulder. But the cause of the failure, investigation disclosed, was in the work of a completely inexperienced mechanic, to whom a hitherto reliable garage had entrusted a recent checkup. The manpower shortage can be inconvenient in such things as laundry service, but it is murderous in the garages.

200

Sunday . . . August 22

A book and a letter caught up with me today, from a fellow named Jerry Ryan. The book is a magazine promotion piece, but the thought behind the sending of it is just about as nice a compliment as this Diarist has had. It grew out of a fellow-feeling for restraint and economy in the use of words. Shake!

Monday . . . August 23

The week starts badly. First, my editor gently pins my ears back for approving the designation "kidnaper" for an agency man who conspires to carry off accounts while drawing pay for shepherding them. Then three publishers of comics exhale various degrees of concern over my comment on their non-use of the continuity technique: one to prove that he does use it (to whom my apologies); one to prove that he shouldn't; and one to suggest that it is contrary to the freedom of the advertising press for me to express an opinion on it. I am feeling slightly crushed.

Tuesday . . . August 24

Hearing that I was going to be in the Southwest, a friend in Simon and Schuster sent me a copy of their recent publication, *An Invitation to Spanish*. I can highly recommend it to anybody who wants an entertaining preparation for post-war Hispano-American relations. After studying it, I decided today to give myself a tryout by ordering breakfast in a Spanish restaurant. So, in my best manner, I asked for jugo de naranja, dos huevos revueltos, pan tostado, y cafe, and was delighted when I was understood. At least, I appeared to be, for the waitress came right back with that old Spanish phrase: "Hokay!"

Wednesday . . . August 25

It is hard enough, in the best of times, to sit down when the peaches are ripening, and write an ad that will strike the mood of Christmas. But who can help the poor copywriter this year, as he cocks his ear to catch the tune which the war gods will be calling four months hence?

Thursday . . . August 26

I have had several experiences with the Federal Trade Commission in my career of crime, and have always come out of them with something less than feelings of mutual regard. So I was jolted today when I discovered that an urbane and delightful gentleman, with whom I had become quite chummy, was the first chairman of this omniscient body, in the days of Woodrow Wilson. Almost he convinces me that a Federal Trade Commissioner, and even an Examiner, may be among God's children.

Friday . . . August 27

Today a client asked me to help him produce, for

202

his organization, a sort of economic primer about his business. He wants to show: (1) what the place of this business is in the total scheme of things; (2) how it came to be, and what its success depends on; (3) the parts played in it by the different groups of workers, the management, and capital; and so on. It is a job that I approach with relish. If there is any hope at all for maintaining an industrial democracy in this country, it is because business men like this one are seeing that everybody in a business has a stake in it.

Saturday . . . August 28

A good deal has been said and written about the news approach in advertising. But visiting today with a young father, I had brought home to me again how much of advertising news is what you need to know when you need to know it. The Greek philosopher who said that we never step twice in the same stream would have understood that the flow of a market is the only constant thing about it. The old news becomes fresh news to somebody, as this flow carries us along to new areas of experience, new needs, and a new receptivity.

Sunday . . . August 29

Whether this world is getting better or worse I wouldn't care to specify. But, for whatever it signifies, I do observe in this country many signs of a greatly increased interest in good art. Many of the artists whom I have known, other than commercial illustrators, formerly lived in genteel poverty. But now quite a few of them make comfortable livelihoods, and can look their grocers in the face. George Hill, with his usual acumen, was among the first in advertising to sense this change in art appreciation.

Monday . . . August 30

Talked with a man who has made his living selling high-priced but mediocre art to the rich. He says that nowadays the newly rich, and especially those in the small towns and western states, are his best picking. The older rich are hugging their decreased incomes to their chests; but the newer rich are still anxious to establish themselves as patrons of the arts and of learning. For them he puts on a regular J. Rufus Wallingford front, complete with Rolls Royce, cane and spats.

Tuesday . . . August 31

Just after contemplating the rows of cabbages in my garden this evening, I saw a Morton's salt ad offering a booklet which would tell me how to make sauerkraut. Now that's what I call intelligent wartime advertising—good for me, good for the country, and good for the advertiser.

204

September, 1943

Wednesday . . . September 1

Had a letter from my boy who is flying overseas for the Army Transport Command. Here are the highlights of one trip as he gives them: Catching a big trout during a layover in Labrador, and cooking it over a campfire "in the grandest forest you ever saw"; watching the sunrise gild the precipitous tops of the great ice cap, sticking up to 12,000 feet through the clouds over Greenland; seeing a big convoy marching across the sea, as orderly as a group of soldiers; popping out of a low cloud, smack on top of a litter of subs around a mother ship, and making a mad scramble for the flare pistol to answer their blinker challenge before they started shooting; cussing the Germans for playing Victrola records of "Deep in the Heart of Texas" on the same frequency as needed radio beams; fighting flies in Africa, in a temperature of 110, with the snow-clad Atlas mountains in sight . . . Be seeing you, Odysseus.

Thursday . . . September 2

A correspondent says that he gets lots of good ideas for advertisers, but has never been able to sell

205

them, and wants me to tell him how to go about it. I have never seen many people make a success of selling ideas only. What the world wants is ideas translated into concrete things and services. Ideas seem to be most salable when they are given as a plus with something a man is going to buy anyhow.

Friday . . . September 3

Watched my wife going through the current issue of *Life*, looking at every picture and reading every caption. Pretty soon I heard her chuckling over a picture and caption in a cold cream ad. When she had turned the page I asked her what it was about, and her answer indicated that to her it was just another editorial picture, interesting in itself, and having no commercial significance. In this instance, at least, the advertiser, by following *Life's* technique, got high readability but no selling.

Saturday . . . September 4

Picked my Elephant Heart plums, and carried a lug of them to the missus, to make her eyes pop. This plum, the last creation of the great Luther Burbank, seems still to be a rarity among fruits, as I never see it on the market. Mine grow to be as big as an ordinary peach, but heart shaped; and it is this, with their blood red flesh, which justifies their name. Good eating.

Sunday . . . September 5

Counting up my blessings in this year of war and

shortages, I listed on the material side the foods with which we had been able to supply ourselves: beef, bacon, hams, lard, milk, cream, butter, cheese, eggs, fryers, turkeys, berries, melons, cherries, apricots, peaches, plums, pears, apples, and all green vegetables. All I need now is a grist mill like Mickey McHugh's to be nearly self-sustaining.

Monday . . . September 6

Made a list of the repair and improvement jobs on my home which have had to be postponed until the war is won. They totaled up to a good many man-days for the building trades and suppliers. Has any magazine in the home field surveyed this accumulating backlog of post-war work? If there are many home owners with needs like mine building up, such a study would have a national as well as trade significance.

Tuesday . . . September 7

One of my associates, who is a member of the School Board in his community, tells me that eight of the teachers who had been hired failed to show up when school began. Higher pay war jobs had gotten them. Here is the kind of thing where the local committees behind the campaign for womanpower can get down to brass tacks. There must be plenty of married teachers who could be induced to come back on the job by a little well directed local advertising.

207

Wednesday . . . September 8

Every once in a while I notice some ad man getting too big for his breeches. Some kind of recognition comes to him which makes him begin to think of himself as a Publicist, an Educator, a Distribution Economist, or whatnot, capitalized. It can't be done, brother. The mark of your trade is upon you. Your strength is there, and if you are shorn of it you will be another Samson. But as that trade gains more and more respect, so will you.

Thursday . . . September 9

Toward the shank of the day, caught the Governor of our state off duty, and we had a little snifter together while he told me of the cares of office in war time. This morning he was gotten out of bed by a lady who telephoned him to please have a dead horse removed from the highway in front of her estate, at once. This was followed by a call from another lady, recently moved into the state, who thought maybe the Governor's wife might get her a cook. A good part of the rest of the day had been spent in long distance telephoning, at his own expense, to persuade the medical authorities who control a rare new drug to furnish some of it for the dying husband of a woman constituent. Votes for women?

Friday . . . September 10

Saw in the New York *Times* an agency's own advertisement which interested me. It gave, in very compact form, an exposition of the copy appeals which this agency has found most effective. Strangely, such material seems to have very little interest for most advertisers. No glamor to it. Just sales.

Saturday . . . September 11

One of the tires on my truck blew out as I was going into town early this morning with a load of fruit. Fortunately, the local rationing board was in session, and quickly agreed that a food supplier should have a new tire. But then I discovered that their permit was only a hunting license. There was not a truck tire of my size in town, and none expected. Continuing my hunt in the next county seat, I finally found a tire in one place and a tube in another. And so to home, at sundown, with the day lost, my gasoline ration reduced, my temper frayed, and my thoughts unkind for Mr. Jeffers.

Sunday . . . September 12

The papers say our boys have landed at Ostia, the port of ancient Rome. I spent a day there once, exploring the ruins with an Italian archaeologist. He had the gift, that man, for making the past come alive. Through his eyes I saw the teeming quays, the merchants busy with their bales, the sailors with harlots hanging on their arms, the Roman Legionnaires coming home, the taverns, the travelers, and all the bustle of a waterfront town. Just words.

Monday . . . September 13

Those OPA gas snoopers must be corrupting the

citizenry down in Florida, for now a reader from there wants to know how come that wrecked car of mine was on that winding mountain road. All right, fellow, I guess it's a fair question: the car was on duty with a secret research operation of the armed forces.

Tuesday . . . September 14

Received a letter from an unknown woman which started as follows: "Dear Sir:—My son, age 24, is sentenced to die in the electric chair on September 17." I submit it for the record as an opening sentence that will come as near to insuring an attentive reading as any ever written. It may have been a cry direct from a woman's heart; but it sounded just a little too professional to me.

Wednesday . . . September 15

A little while back I recorded that I was ordering another supply of my favorite pipe tobacco from England, and predicted that it would come through in spite of hell and high water. Today it did, two pounds of it, in hermetically sealed quarter-pound tins. In the same mail was a letter from an English advertising man, telling me how the post-war slogan of English business has become "Export or Die."

Thursday . . . September 16

Had a letter from L. P. Finley, of the Union Fork & Hoe Company (whose products I have used for years), expressing his hope that this Diary will be published in book form. Very nice of him. On this subject the ayes seem to have it, and I have just finished forking over the first year's crop of these jottings, to prepare them for immortality. But Lord, how I hate to read the stuff myself!

Friday . . . September 17

Having occasion to look up the dictionary definition of economics, I was reminded of one I received one night around a campfire in the Arizona desert. There were four of us: a Jewish trader of the country, his 18-year old son, a Texas cattle buyer, and this tenderfoot. The trader had been good enough to give me a lift in his wheezy Model T when I had missed the mail stage for a point 80 miles from the railroad. But night had overtaken us on the slow desert track, and the car's lights failing to work, we lay down in the sage brush until morning. Getting cold toward dawn, I got up and made a greasewood fire, and soon the others joined me. While the coffee boiled and the stars paled, the trader's son told me of his ambition to go to college and study economics. At that the trader pricked up his ears. "What is that economics?" he asked. When we had tried to explain he was silent a minute. Then he said: "Well, I tell you all the economics you need to know: just milk the fellow what does the milking." Then to me: "What business you in? Advertising? That's the kind! *You* milk the fellow what does the milking!"

Saturday . . . September 18

Visited with a man who, a few years ago, had one of the most prosperous women's wear businesses in Germany. He was worth at that time some $2,000,-000, and had a quarter million of it in gold certificates in a Holland bank. But in Hitler's anti-Semitic squeeze he lost it all, and felt lucky to escape to this country with his family and $3,000. Today, at 68, with his sons in our Army, he and his daughter have re-established themselves as successful designers and producers of smart sports wear, and are on their way up again.

Sunday . . . September 19

That Palomino, painted by Fred Ludekins for this week's *Post* cover, makes my heart leap. My Pal is getting old, and will soon have to go to his last pasture. But somewhere there is another of these Golden Horses which I must have.

Monday . . . September 20

I wonder if there isn't a story waiting for somebody to tell, in advertising, for the Railway Express Agency. If I had been asked, a short time ago, to name an unimaginative monopoly, I suspect this Agency might have been my choice—if I had thought of it at all. But some recent experiences have enlightened me. In fact, it looks to me now as though this might be the smartest outfit in any branch of the transportation business, with a service attitude that is inadequately appreciated by the public.

212

Tuesday . . . September 21

My first business transaction, at the age of nine, was to take a penny given me by my mother, invest it in two copies of an evening newspaper, and sell them for a penny each. When I found that capital could thus be doubled in a day it was like discovering a gold mine. Thereafter I sold papers every afternoon, after school, until I got a regular job in a publishing business at the age of twelve. No doubt the laws prohibiting child labor were necessary and have done more good than harm, but I cannot help wondering about them during this manpower shortage. I know they would have prevented my getting a lot of useful education. But then I had the good luck to do my child-laboring in that most educational of all enterprises, a printing house.

Wednesday . . . September 22

Picked up a copy of *Look* on a newsstand, with a strong picture of Willkie on the cover. "There," said a stranger next to me, "is our next president." "What makes you think so?" I asked. "Because," said he, "I am a traveling man, and wherever I go Willkie is the fellow people are talking about." He wasn't traveling for Mike Cowles either.

Thursday . . . September 23

It is said that Roy Howard once instructed Scripps-Howard editors somewhat as follows: "When you want to attack a man don't call him li-

213

belous names. Just tell what he did in such a way that the reader will say: 'Why, the dirty so-and-so!' " The suggestion holds good for ad writers. Don't praise the product. Just tell what it does, and how it does it, so that the reader will say: "I must try that." In short, go light on the adjectives and heavy on the verbs.

Friday . . . September 24

Winston Churchill's endorsement of Basic English has given it the kind of popular attention its compilers have long sought. It must be nearly twenty years ago that one of its promoters asked me to introduce its use into advertising; and I still have the dozen or more books about it which I accumulated at that time. I, too, believe that it is the best tool that has been devised for facilitating international communication. But I quit experimenting with it for advertising when I found that Poe's tale, "The Gold Bug," translated into Basic becomes "The Gold Insect." Advertising needs more color and nuance than that.

Saturday . . . September 25

A drizzly, gusty, equinoctial day, so used it to give my study a housecleaning—my wife and maids having been warned not to touch it on pain of death. Got all my bookshelves in order, all my files purged of bygones, and all my catalogs, pamphlets, clippings, and other fugitive material neatly classified in new folders. Tonight I am feeling too virtuous to live with.

214

Sunday . . . September 26

No frost yet, and the rain has blown away, so to-morrow we will make hay while the sun shines and start on our fourth cutting of alfalfa. Let's see: better than five tons to the acre at $30 a ton . . . why, there's millions in it!

Monday . . . September 27

Saw a copy of a very sane and wise letter about war advertising which was sent to every member of the Association of National Advertisers by Charlie Mortimer, its chairman. I do not see how any advertiser who reads it can be in doubt as to where and how he may make a contribution to the war effort in keeping with his business interests. And any advertiser who didn't receive it can, I understand, get a copy by asking ANA for it. There are still a lot who apparently don't understand that advertising which brags about their war contributions is not itself a contribution.

Tuesday . . . September 28

A gentleman who is a magazine writer wants to know how he can start a mail order business in his home, with a few hundred dollars' capital and no experience. It has been done. I know a girl who did it with her grandmother's recipes for some very tasty preserves. But I never knew it to be done by anybody who did not first have a product he believed in. The fact that a good product comes first, and that

215

advertising, mail order, or otherwise is only part of the mechanics of distribution for it, has escaped quite a few observers—and practitioners.

Wednesday . . . September 29

Noticed an advertisement of a conservative New York investment house, headed "Go West Young Dollars," featuring a booklet about their belief in the future of Pacific Coast industries. Having been a bull on that empire for some twenty years or more I must applaud their vision. But, Lord, how long it takes to get some minds across the Hudson River!

Thursday . . . September 30

How revealing a letter can be! I have one today from a complete stranger, applying for a job. On the face of his record he is a man of high calibre, worth sitting down with for better acquaintance. But there are a dozen little things about this letter—in the stationery itself, in the points of view, in the approach, and the expressions used—which spell nothing but pompous ass.

October, 1943

Friday . . . October 1

Talked with the chairman of our local draft board about the deferment of a key man in our business. He did not give me much hope. But every time I have an experience like this I am impressed anew with what a lot of fine citizens we have in this country, doing these mean local board jobs as faithfully as they can. In fact, I must count as one of the gains from this war the greater appreciation I have of the qualities hidden in hitherto casually-known neighbors.

Saturday . . . October 2

Took into town a truck load of extra fancy Grimes Golden apples, just off the trees, and sold them to a chain store buyer. The price made me feel like a profiteer. But when Chet Bowles' ceiling on them goes into effect next week I'll probably be cussing him out.

Sunday . . . October 3

Reviewed the financial situation for the year to date of two institutions, scientific and cultural, with which I am connected. Neither has any endowment nor any state support, and at the beginning of this year it was believed by many that financial contributions would so dwindle that the doors of these institutions might have to be closed. Instead, each has received more support than it did in the same period last year. Apparently we have made up our minds that such institutions are also among the things we are fighting to preserve.

Monday . . . October 4

Most of us were shown in our youth how we could accumulate a competency through a lifetime of modest savings multiplied by compound interest. But I know a man who has demonstrated that the same procedure will produce a mental competency as well. For over thirty years he has steadily devoted the spare hours from a busy advertising life to painstaking work and original research in the field of public health. Today he is probably the outstanding layman in this field, and has enriched his own life while saving many others. And now he has retired from business with an inexhaustible fund in his intellectual bank. A salute to Bill Groom!

Tuesday . . . October 5

An old friend says that I revealed my authorship of this Diary by recording here a story which I told him in 1927. But he promises he won't tell. He would be more than human (which he isn't!) if he doesn't.

218

When one reader in Canada recently speculated about my identity in a letter to the editor, he received an anonymous post card from New York revealing it. If you want something widely circulated, whisper it.

Wednesday . . . October 6

Today I can sympathize with Montgomery Ward's report on what it has cost them to send back the mail orders for catalog goods which they couldn't supply. A mail piece of mine which went out two weeks ago has already produced twice the number of expected orders, and the advertiser is hopping mad at me. We will have to revise our notions of a normal response while this goods vacuum holds.

Thursday . . . October 7

I think I may read as many magazines as any man living, but the one which I really savor is a publication with only 30,000 circulation. In it I absorb the advertising almost as part of the editorial content, and am, I feel sure, more responsive to it there than elsewhere. Such publications invariably cost more per thousand than the extensive circulations, but I am not sure that the greater depth of their circulations does not make them worth it.

Friday . . . October 8

In a recent issue *Time* spoke of the "bumbling" Business Advisory Council (of the Department of

Commerce). An instructive example of how the epithet often makes color at the expense of accuracy. Among the "bumblings" of this little publicized Council are: (1) the projection into the Washington scene of a score or more top flight business men, including Ed Stettinius, the new Under Secretary of State; Averell Harriman, the new Ambassador to Russia; and Will Clayton, Assistant Secretary of Commerce; and (2) the initial sponsoring of the postwar Committee for Economic Development, including the furnishing of its chairman, Paul Hoffman—whom *Time* recently extolled.

Saturday . . . October 9

Busy all day in the warm October glow, getting my Golden Delicious apples off the trees. Made every picker wear white cotton gloves, and found the psychological effect of these greatly reduced the number of culls due to carelessness in handling.

Sunday . . . October 10

A friend in England writes me that it is now said there that of all the weeds those easiest to get rid of are a widow's. All that is required is to say *Wilt thou* and they *wilt*. But behind this typical piece of English humor is a situation that is no joke. Population students are predicting that the entire western world will find itself with a post-war surplus of women, with many significant social changes as a result.

220

Monday . . . October 11

My barber, who was originally a Missouri farm boy, has always been rabidly anti-English. Today I discovered the source of his feelings. As a doughboy in the last war he visited London, and called on a prosperous English business man to whom he had a letter of introduction from a brother back in Missouri. The Englishman's first remark on seeing him was: "Why would my brother give you, a common soldier, a letter of introduction to *me?*" My barber friend did not know that there is a type of Londoner who apes the gentleman without his education and gentleness.

Tuesday . . . October 12

A publisher does not like to change a successful business formula any more than other men, so resistance to paper rationing is natural. But so far as advertising is concerned, I think we could learn to do with a good deal less paper than we now use, with no great loss of power. Before me are two copies of the same advertisement—one in a full page in the New York *Times*, the other in a full page, tabloid size. For the life of me I cannot see that the one using half the paper required by the other is any the less effective.

Wednesday . . . October 13

Heard a woman complaining because, when she gave her cook an increase in wages, the girl promptly spent it on such things as a hair-do and some expensive camera portraits. Reminds me of some country gentlemen neighbors who used to sit around on their porch of a summer day, sipping mint juleps and talking about how lazy the WPA pick-and-shovel men were.

Thursday . . . October 14

Shocked when I got the preparation bills on some ads I had turned out. Upon investigation discovered their high figures were due to the same old trouble: namely, letting the art man put in a lot of fancy strokes which called for extra engraving and printing costs. Nine times out of ten these add nothing to the selling power of the message.

Friday . . . October 15

A few days ago I hired a boy of nineteen, who had been rejected by the Army on his eyesight. He is the son of a coal miner, and since finishing the ninth grade in school has been working at the job of picking stone out of the coal. But I haven't seen a kid for a long time with as much ambition and git-up-and-go. Thank God there is still such yeast in the American dough.

Saturday . . . October 16

In the Oxford English Dictionary the phrase "fall of the year" is noted only as a United States usage. Contrasted with the pale English "autumn" it offers one good example of the greater vividness of our speech. Many others may be found in Mencken's great compilation on "The American Language," and a thoughtful student of it can see there how these differences in words often embalm some of our differences in ideas and outlook.

Sunday . . . October 17

Picked out the turkey destined to grace my Thanksgiving board, and shut it up for fattening and tenderizing. The farmer has his troubles in war-time, even as other men, but in many ways he is certainly a man with special privileges. As one myself (skeptics to the contrary), I have so far escaped the rigors of both food and gasoline rationing almost entirely; and have found that I can buy many things which, as an ad man, I would not be permitted to purchase. Find I can even bid for one of those hogs lost on a bet by the Governor of Nebraska to the Governor of our state, and contributed by him to the National War Fund.

Monday . . . October 18

Because their milline rate is high, the small town and rural weeklies do not get much attention from the generality of national advertisers. But they still have plenty of political significance, as every Congressman knows. So I was interested today to note in one of them—a mouthpiece of a Democratic state

223

regime—an editorial advising this state party to dissociate itself from the national administration if it wanted to win the next election.

Tuesday . . . October 19

Received from the Treasury a form letter asking for criticism of the advertising activities in the recent war bond campaign, and for constructive suggestions for the fourth campaign which is coming. It seems to me that we are still not getting enough of the money from the wage earning groups to whom most of this advertising is supposedly directed. I suspect that one reason is that we have not yet *concreted* the proposition sufficiently. Maybe I could get more excited over lending Uncle Sam a gun to kill a Jap than I could over lending him more dollars for a piece of paper.

Wednesday . . . October 20

One of the greatest schools of advertising ever conducted was the old *System Magazine*, when owned and run by Arch Shaw. He made a house organ into a million dollar publishing property, very largely through his instinct for mail selling and promotion. And in the process he made a dozen or more young fellows of 1910 into some of the top advertising and publishing men of today. The last time I saw Shaw he was immersed in economic and political studies; but I found that he could still r'ar up like an old fire horse over a key sheet of direct selling returns.

Thursday . . . October 21

In our town the National War Fund is being responded to through a sense of duty by the responsible citizens, reluctantly by the partisans of the different local and national organizations participating, and hardly at all by the general populace. The people who set this scheme up nationally were well versed in the mechanics of fund raising, but they called in the advertising and publicity people too late to give the program the sharp emotional appeal it needs for popular response. Another failure to recognize that advertising begins with the shaping of the product itself.

Friday . . . October 22

When I see the way in which men of diverse interests are working together in the War Advertising Council, I wonder whether competition is the natural instinct of man that it is cracked up to be. Maybe the cooperative state yields more actual satisfaction than we have been accustomed to think; and that the competitive drive is largely a by-product of the industrial revolution and the division of labor.

Saturday . . . October 23

Spent the evening by a purring wood fire, rereading the immortal "Adventures of Huckleberry Finn."

225

Huck is the world's greatest example of the educational superiority of doing and observing over book larnin', and he always does my soul good.

Sunday . . . October 24

Speaking of book larnin', I notice that President Hutchins of the University of Chicago is going to give his famous course in the One Hundred Best Books to a special group of Upper Case Chicago citizens. Sounds to me like one of Bill Benton's ideas —especially when I note that the publication and sale of a University of Chicago edition of these books is to follow.

Monday . . . October 25

A teacher of business correspondence wants to know what kind of letterhead <u>indicated</u> to me a "pompous ass." I could be specific about this one case, but would that be of any real use? What we *are* has a way of shining through whatever we say or do; and I am afraid that pomposity is a disease which cannot be cured by attempting to eradicate its symptoms in a letterhead. It will only break out again in some other manifestation.

Tuesday . . . October 26

Making bricks without straw is no novelty assignment for the copywriter, but the worst case I ever had was when I was asked, quite a few years ago,

226

to do overnight a series of ads on shotguns. At that time I had never owned such a gun, nor shot one. So I was in a pretty how-to-do. In desperation I got out a couple of years' files of all the outdoor magazines, and spent the night going through their articles and their questions-and-answers departments, tabulating all the things their readers seemed to want to know about shotguns. Out of this expert material I built a series of informative ads which proved to be highly successful. I do not recommend such quick-lunch methods as ideal, but this case taught me never to be afraid of any subject, as long as a good library was available.

Wednesday . . . October 27

Boredom with life is so widespread a disease that I reckon the first big job we have to do in advertising is to be interesting. There is a nice point in every ad where interest must be transmuted into desire, but that is another subject. To succeed in catching interest, in the face of all our competition, is in itself a big achievement, and some day I want to write a book about it. I have a feeling that the problem is more involved than is indicated by the over-simplified diagrams of the advertising textbooks. That it is rooted in the writer's cultivation of his own capacities for becoming interested in anything.

Thursday . . . October 28

Spent some time today with a man who has the

most amazing memory I have ever known. This, combined with wide reading, has given him a reputation for intelligence which his actions do not sustain. I have noticed that a good many wearers of scholarship keys have the same kind of gifts—our older educational methods having apparently favored the effortless memorizers. The most intelligent possessor of such a key that I know bought his in a pawnshop, and solemnly wears it to gatherings of distinguished associates who know that he never went to college.

Friday . . . October 29

Arthur Brisbane used to say that if you listened in on any conversation in the subways you would find most of it made up of "He said—" and "She said—." Not many advertisers seem to recognize this pervasiveness of interest in the concrete personality. The corporate "we" and the copywriter's third person "they" will never have the pull of "I" to "you."

Saturday . . . October 30

At the farm to see the first snow flurry speckle the fields. The crops all in or sold; the woodshed filled; the cold cellar stocked; and the fallen leaves being gathered to the compost pit. This year I am trying the mixing of these leaves with Adco, the artificial manure maker developed at Rothamsted, England, the oldest agricultural experiment station in the

228

world, where records on the maintenance of soil fertility in one field have been kept for a hundred years.

Sunday . . . October 31

Spent a broken night in a small town hotel, and got up feeling like a sore-headed bear. Some day I hope to find a hotel proprietor who makes a business of selling sleep, and runs his house for that purpose. In a big city the individual night noises are blended into a hum that is not too disturbing; but in the quiet of the smaller towns two loud-mouthed taxi drivers and one garbage can banger can ruin a night. Maybe Ed Ahrens can start a crusade about this.

November, 1943

Monday . . . November 1

I see by the papers that the Treasury estimates it
received thirty-six million dollars' worth of advertising and publicity support for the 3rd War Loan.
That is undoubtedly the greatest concentration of
advertising power ever developed in such a brief period. A. D. Lasker once told me that it took him
years to learn that mere volume of advertising could
be as important as the copy message. This enormous
bond promotion seems to support the idea, when it
is calculated that this thirty-six million of space and
time is only a fraction of 1% of the nineteen billion
of sales resulting.

Tuesday . . . November 2

Talked with a man who has made his living selling investments in property for chain store occu-
pancy. According to his figures, money put into land
and buildings leased to a chain like Woolworth,
Kresge, Penney, etc., is a better bet than stock in the
same companies—the income being more assured
and a hedge against inflation better provided for. I
am always intrigued when I discover a new, special-

230

ized function like this man's in our complex economy. It adds to my belief that the ingenuity of the millions, stirred by private profit, is more effectively functional than the planning of a few master minds.

Wednesday . . . November 3

Every publisher now seems to be wrestling with the formulation of a policy for rationing the amount of advertising space he has left to sell. It would be an easier job if he had only advertisers to satisfy, but he can't ignore the ambitions of his salesmen and the agencies. Not having the problem, it is easy for me to be dogmatic about it. I would give first priority to the advertisers with merchandise and services to sell; second to the advertisers, new or old, with a genuine war service message; third to the advertisers who have demonstrated a consistent purpose to maintain or build a postwar reputation. Away down at the bottom I would put those advertisers who are obviously squandering tax money on unmitigated bellywash.

Thursday . . . November 4

Talked with a highly successful business man who was bemoaning the fact that he couldn't devote more of the remainder of his life to "public service." I find this a rather common affliction among men in their fifties who have reached a certain position. It makes me wonder what is wrong with our business structure. Certainly a well-run business is in itself a public service, as valuable to its community and its customers as it is to its owners. Why isn't it completely satisfying to the man who guides it? Perhaps because in our society we don't have any way of honoring industrial statesmanship, as the English do by knighthood.

Friday . . . November 5

Heard a banker make a speech in which he referred with scorn to the lushness of current advertising expenditures, and to the smell of escaping tax money attached to them. Maybe this paper rationing will be a blessing in disguise, if it puts some brakes on this particular area of advertising expenditures.

Saturday . . . November 6

Spent the day in Washington, and found the belief very prevalent there that the climax of the European war is at hand. One result is that the business men there, tired of the slings and arrows of outrageous government, are turning their thoughts homeward. This worries one key industrialist there above all else. He says the radicals are just waiting for this to happen, so that they can take over the industrial controls which will have to be kept on, in the reconversion from war to peace.

Sunday . . . November 7

I wonder how many advertising directors and sales managers are giving any thought to the export

232

field in their post-war planning? By and large, our industries have never really become "foreign trade conscious." Yet we are coming out of this war with the greatest merchant marine the world has ever seen—England currently having 40,000 men building ships and we 800,000. To keep that fleet in being, and perhaps to make the difference between success and failure in full employment, we will need a great expansion in our foreign commerce.

Monday . . . November 8

With all this shortage of manpower to deal with an increased volume of advertising, why don't we repeat more ads, instead of manufacturing new ones for every insertion? If an ad is a good one it can stand a lot more circulation and repetition than most ever get; and some of the shrewdest and most successful advertisers have proved that such repetition pays. An agency is always loath to recommend this practice for fear it won't seem to be earning its salt. But right now advertisers would make a great contribution to the whole supply situation, to their own benefit, if they would encourage this idea, both in space and in radio commercials.

Tuesday . . . November 9

In New York I went into a store of one of the biggest grocery chains and found only the scrubbiest kind of apples for sale. When I inquired why they had no good ones, I was told they were all in black market hands. This, apparently, is the result of putting a price ceiling on apples which makes no allowance for varieties or grades, so that the poorest apples fetch as much as the best. That doesn't make sense to an apple knocker like me, Chet.

Wednesday . . . November 10

Some days I feel so radical that I wish the paper shortage would force us all to do away completely with white space in ads, and make us put everything into straight reading matter form. That might make us see that it is only the inherent interest of the story that counts, and that all the beautiful art work, trick layouts, and typographical styling in the world won't make an advertising sow's ear into a silk purse.

Thursday . . . November 11

Interviewed a gushing young thing who wanted a job because she "just loved to write." If she had said "loved to have written" I might have thought she knew what she was talking about. But nobody really loves to write, because writing is thinking; and thinking is the most loathsome form of work.

Friday . . . November 12

Senator Truman's speech before the Western Council of the Four A's was a good example of how an open-minded man can educate himself when he really gets down to it. But, Lord, how painful it is to

234

sit through these voyages of discovery! I wonder how the Senator would like to have me bone up on the political theory behind Congressional investigations, and then take the time of his committee to expound it.

Saturday . . . November 13

Talked with a shrewd observer of editorial material who thinks that the dullest part of most newspapers is their business sections. He thinks they could be as exciting as the sports pages, if their editors could only see the personalities and competitive struggles behind the business statistics. And where, he asks, is the columnist who has done for the business pages what Pegler, Runyan, Kieran *et al.* did for sports?

Sunday . . . November 14

Took my Airedale for an after-dark stroll, and had him leave me with rocket gun suddenness for an alfalfa field which we were skirting. Heard a light patter of hoof beats in the night, and raised my flashlight just in time to see five graceful deer go over the stone wall and up a hillside. Marked the spot as "Unrationed Point."

Monday . . . November 15

Not long ago I recorded here some observations on the sensitivity of Congressmen to small town newspapers. The Bankhead bill, appropriating $15,-000,000 of the taxpayers' money for advertising handouts to such papers, proves the point. One Senator who voted for this racket admitted privately that it was all wrong, but said he couldn't withstand the pressure from these small papers in his state. The publishers who are back of this pressure are doing advertising a great disservice in promoting its use by government on this political basis. And doing themselves a great disservice, too, in the unfavorable attention they are attracting among legitimate advertisers.

Tuesday . . . November 16

I have recently had an opportunity to note the results from two campaigns—one in newspapers and one in magazines—where the advertisers have been persuaded to stick to one theme and one style of presentation for more than two years. There is evidence in each case that the impact of the advertising on its public has steadily increased in force. We too often underestimate the value of such continuity. Advertisers who wouldn't think of changing a radio personality, or the product personality projected through a package, will switch their printed advertising personality so often that nobody has a chance to feel intimate with them.

Wednesday . . . November 17

Had an evening of good talk with a man who has undertaken one of the most interesting assignments I ever heard of. He is out to explore, for a distin-

236

guished group, how the processes of invention and discovery are speeded up or retarded in a modern society. In essence, this is to determine what produces the largest number of creative men, and what encourages them to function. He can range far and deep on that one—as our conversation did.

Thursday . . . November 18

One of the questions which came up in my friend's conversation last night was whether the really big corporations remain creative, or whether they tend to get "sot in their ways." Had an experience in point today, which I hope was not typical. For months I have been trying to make one very large corporation see the potential in one sideline of their business. This afternoon I was told that their directors admit that the possibilities are probably there, but have decided to hope that somebody else will develop them. Too tired, it seems, to do it themselves. Yet I have heard the same men damn the New Dealer who contends that business will no longer do the risk-taking that a dynamic society must have.

Friday . . . November 19

It was Herbert Spencer, I think, who told of the consternation with which an English reform organization received the news that Parliament had passed a bill for which it had fought for twenty years or so. That left the organization with nothing to do and nowhere to go. We are due to see the same phenomenon in many war agencies, public and private, and their efforts toward self-perpetuation will be instructive and amusing to watch. They ought to get in touch with the Association of Trade Association Executives, whose members are experts in devising fresh issues worth fighting for.

Saturday . . . November 20

Ran into Ed Noble, the Life Savers king and Blue Network mogul. As soon as the war is over I would like to see Ed given a contract to operate the United States Government. He would have us out of the red in no time.

Sunday . . . November 21

Some years ago, at a dinner in England, I sat next to a man who conducted a successful children's program on the BBC. In the course of the evening I discovered that he was also a baronet, an archaeologist, and the author of a history of India—the kind of range one so often finds among educated Englishmen. Browsing through my bookshelves this afternoon I ran across the copy of his history which he had sent me, and for the first time felt an inclination to read it. Found it a scholarly performance which illustrated why we are sometimes handicapped in dealing with Englishmen on world affairs.

Monday . . . November 22

Attended a meeting to discuss what could be done

238

to defeat the Bankhead bill. Some there thought it had gone so far in Congress that any fight was hopeless, and we were bound to be licked; therefore nothing should be done. This bill has in it the seeds of destruction for the whole advertising and publishing industry as we know it, and if we take it lying down we shall deserve it. Even its passage by the Senate need not be taken as final there. I once had the pleasure of helping raise such a stink about a bill that had been so passed that it was recalled for another vote and killed.

Tuesday . . . November 23

Running through an old book on English composition I came across the ancient schoolmaster's injunction:
"And don't confound the language of the nation
With long-tailed words in *osity* and *ation*."
With a change from "language" to "the people of the nation" this might well be posted in every copy crib.

Wednesday . . . November 24

In from the farm came His Majesty the Gobbler, fattened to a full twenty pounds of double breasted perfection. The butcher who undertook to dress him for the basting pan nearly cried when he parted with him, and made several sly suggestions of a black market character. But I lugged him home again like any Pilgrim Father, and tucked him away in the cooler along with the bottle of *Berncastler Doktor* designed to wash him down.

Thursday . . . *November 25*

For my sins in putting off the evil day I had to spend most of this Thanksgiving one preparing for a speech whose delivery date is almost upon me. Every year, on New Year's Day, I highly resolve that I will indulge no more in this futile sport. Then somebody catches me in a weak and vain moment, and I fall. The time required for such auto-intoxicating exercises is out of all proportion to the benefits conferred or received.

Friday . . . *November 26*

All week I have been entertained by the nimble verbal gymnastics of the reporters, columnists, and editorial writers in dealing with what is called "the forthcoming Big Three conference." If anybody ever succeeded in making love without mentioning love these fellows have. And now *Time* outdoes the Book of Revelations with its featured summary of the headlines of the week on this subject.

Saturday . . . *November 27*

Talked with a man who has spent the past couple of years in psychological warfare units, first with the English and latterly with us. Asked him if he felt he had learned anything for advertising from the people in this field. He said, on the contrary, that advertising people were able to teach more than they could learn in this work; and thought that the Eng-

240

lish had been more willing to recognize this than we had been.

Sunday . . . November 28

It won't be long now before we shall be hearing of advertisers and industries that are interested again in expanding the total consumption for their type of product. We have many case histories to prove how advertising can do this kind of job, and we know pretty well how to go about it. But I wonder if we in advertising know as much as we might about pricing as a major element in the elasticity of demand. For what kinds of products would a lower unit price and a lower unit advertising expenditure produce both more sales and more advertising? For what kinds does a lower unit price hurt the product's standing with the public?

Monday . . . November 29

Now the Department of Commerce comes along with the same suggestion recently made here, namely, that many advertisements could be cut down in size without loss in efficiency, and important paper savings thus made. This Department has been a good friend to, and an intelligent observer of, advertising, so this is no New Deal flanking movement. Now, also, I get a letter on this subject from Roy Washburn, long-time agency art director who, as a major in the Army air forces, has been helping prepare their printed instruction material. He says they have learned to get amazing results under space restrictions that would make most art directors throw up their hands. As the bum said to the barkeep, "the way to sell more beer is to sell less foam."

Tuesday . . . November 30

In the earlier days of advertising so much space was kept sold on the plea that the advertiser must look only for "cumulative results," that the phrase finally became one for derision. But it is, in fact, if properly understood, an exact description of the way in which most advertising works. Even in successful mail order advertising the direct and immediate results from a given advertisement are often not sufficient to cover costs and show a profit. But if the advertising and the product make customers who will repeat, the volume eventually accumulated will bring the advertiser out with a profit on the operation. The length of time required for this will depend very largely on (a) how many new customers each ad starts; (b) what percentage of these will repeat; and (c) what the natural rate of consumption and repurchase is for the product involved. For some very slowly or occasionally consumed products you really need to have had your grandfather start the business.

December, 1943

Wednesday . . . December 1

Sat in on a powwow between two men who were on opposite sides of a rather touchy controversial issue. The discussions started in an atmosphere of suspicion and antagonism, but ended in friendliness and mutual respect—even though there was still disagreement on the issue. This was due entirely to the fact that the man on one side had two great qualities: complete candor and unquenchable good humor. You can't beat them in a negotiator.

Thursday . . . December 2

What this country needs more of is guys that will get up in meeting and shout "Nonsense!" So when George Wright of Baltimore did just that about an item recently recorded here I was glad to learn there was another stout fellow in the house. Still, I hope you will permit me a *little* exaggeration now and then, George. It is such a comfort to write some copy that won't be viewed with an FTC squint.

243

Tonight I read an article by Dorothy Thompson in the current issue of *Life* which I am going to clip for my files of advertising literature. It deals with the problem of what our treatment of a defeated Germany is to be. But it exhibits more clearly and dramatically than anything else I can recall at the moment how completely the actions of people are determined by the *ideas* they hold; and how without an idea to be loyal to, their lives produce chaos. For people whose job is essentially the implanting of ideas—but who sometimes forget it—this article is good red meat.

Brought in from the farm a huge packing case, full of home-canned peaches, pears, plums, apricots, and cherries—sweet and sour—and stored them away in our city pantry. I don't know whether such an operation is economical, as compared with buying the fine products of the California packers, but I do know that it yields, in Eddie Guest's words, "a heap of living." The pleasure I had in raising and picking these fruits, and that my wife had in canning them, might not lend itself to grade labeling, but there's a lot of it in every jar.

A friend of mine wanted a velocipede for her young daughter, but there were none on the market.

244

I suggested a want ad which got her a perfectly good one, second hand. Today I found in an antique shop that was open for Sunday morning strollers just the child's workbench and tools I had been looking for as a gift for a small boy. I wonder if one more brake on inflation couldn't be fashioned by an organized effort to increase second-hand trading in short goods. Maybe local war bond committees could run a White Elephant shop where all the transactions were payable in stamps and bonds.

Monday . . . December 6

Had lunch with a group of university people who were debating what business subjects, if any, should be included in their curriculum. We were all agreed that the objective of a university education should be a trained and liberal mind, and that this is a more valuable business asset than any smattering of business knowledge. But most of us also thought it possible to teach any subject—including business ones —in a way which does liberate and train the mind, provided the right man be found to teach it! There's the rub.

Tuesday . . . December 7

A while ago I wrote a little mail order ad for a man who has spent a lot of money for space, but seldom in ways from which he could see direct results. When he counted up the dollars from this little venture he said: "It really makes you believe in adver-

245

tising, doesn't it?" The advertising writer who has come up through this hard school of mail order key sheets does have this conviction. He *knows* that advertising can sell; and he knows that *how* you do it does make a whale of a difference. His danger is that he won't go on from there, and carry that knowledge and conviction into the sale of *ideas* about products, which, when they gain mass acceptance, may determine the habits of the nation.

Wednesday . . . December 8

Talked with a big advertiser-in-a-hurry. His postwar business situation is likely to be a most complex one, yet he had the idea that any good agency ought to be able to sit down and pull advertising rabbits out of the hat almost overnight. The fact that some agencies had pretended to do so in speculative solicitations encouraged him in this notion. Yet he wouldn't think of making a comparable expenditure for plant facilities without months of careful architectural and engineering preparations.

Thursday . . . December 9

It seems probable that the reading habit is less well established among big business executives, and especially sales executives, than with any other part of our alert population. Being largely skimmers of printed matter themselves, it is hard for them to accept adequate amounts of "copy" in their printed advertising. They will often accept without question

246

two hundred words of selling in a radio commercial, and gag over fifty words in print. This is, perhaps, the biggest single handicap under which printed advertising labors today.

Friday . . . December 10

Went into a big women's wear store to get my wife a negligee for Christmas. Found myself in a mob of saleswomen, svelte models, and lady customers, with here and there another unhappy oaf like myself. Escaped with the garment and a new simile: As self-conscious as a man in a lingerie shop.

Saturday . . . December 11

A big corporation, in which I happen to own a little stock, sends me a proxy to sign, empowering the management to vote my stock at their annual meeting. Upon examining an accompanying statement I find that they propose to re-elect a board of directors made up entirely of officers and employes, some of whom own no stock at all, and the total of whose holdings is less than 1% of the stock outstanding. I have no reason to doubt either the honesty or efficiency of this management, but it would sit a lot better with me if a few of their board members were men of public standing, not beholden to the management for their jobs.

Sunday . . . December 12

Eric Johnston of the U. S. Chamber of Commerce

has recently highlighted the divergence of views between many English and American business interests over the place of private enterprise in the postwar world. Apparently he was shocked at the acceptance which he found in England for the cartel idea. To refresh my memory on this silent revolution which has been taking place in English business ever since World War I, this afternoon I got out and started to reread Professor Arthur Lucas' book about it: "Industrial Reconstruction and the Control of Competition."

Monday . . . December 13

Anybody who remembers the furious spending of advertising money in 1920, and the cold douche of 1921, is bound to shake his head now and then over the present indifference to the dollar sign. Appropriations, salaries, and collateral expenditures of every sort are now being tossed about in a sort of gay abandonment of ordinary business prudence. Even Treasurers talk about "ten cent dollars," and economy is the most unappealing word in the dictionary. But sad will be the cold, gray dawn of the morning after.

Tuesday . . . December 14

One of the nice distinctions to be made between products is as to which can profit from a background of social prestige, and which need the coloration of authority. Some writers have suggested that any product used in public can profit from social pres-

248

tige, and any product used in private cannot. But this breaks down when one considers, respectively, a lawn mower and a cold cream. A safer rule seems to be that if the product is used in public in relation to one's social status; or if it is used in private as part of the intimate expression of personality; then its social standing will be influential. If, like the lawn mower, it is used in public for purely utilitarian purposes; or, like a dentifrice, is used in private without relation to the dreams of personality; then the authoritative endorsement becomes more potent.

Wednesday . . . December 15

Dined with an English army officer who has recently come here to do a job coordinating some of their and our activities, in preparation for the big push. Asked him what was happening in England since so many of our people were overrunning the place. He said our men were getting along nicely, but that the English were getting fed so much Spam they were getting sick of seeing it, and he believed the overdosage of this one food was rapidly becoming the chief strain on Anglo-American relations.

Thursday . . . December 16

Received with pleasure from a friend in that business two bottles of California wines. This led me to reflect, with some amusement, upon the natural history of the ideas which I have held from time to time about alcoholic beverages, and how these ideas have influenced my consumption of such products. In my youth, I was taught that only whisky (meaning Bourbon) was a gentleman's drink. Beer was German and vulgar. Gin was "nigger poison." And wine (along with women and song) was an ingredient of debauchery. Such deeply implanted, parochial notions were only slowly changed by many different kinds of experience. The last to go was the one about wine, which in the end yielded to European living. But this in turn planted in me a fancy for myself as a vintage connoisseur, which made me sniff at our domestic blends. Only recently did I begin to learn how really good some of these domestic wines are. Still, not *quite* as good as that bottle of Chateau Lafite 1929 which I had last night.

Friday . . . December 17

Listened to a presentation of the plans made by the Treasury for advertising and selling activities in the forthcoming bond drive. These Treasury people have certainly learned how to conduct these drives with all the skill of a revivalist getting sinners to hit the sawdust trail. But there is bound to be a heap of backsliding from such pressure peaks. To keep these bonds sold the Treasury will perhaps have to learn also how the churches keep the sinners in the straight and narrow path.

Saturday . . . December 18

Chico McGillicuddy came home today, after two weeks in a dog hospital. He was waiting for me at

250

the door when I came in tonight. If I could be sure that he would be waiting at the Pearly Gates to greet me with the same frantic joy, I would try harder to insure my arrival there.

Sunday . . . December 19

A Sunday in the city is my idea of a little corner in purgatory. I eat too much, exercise too little, and fudge the homework I know I ought to do. Spent most of this one lying on my back reading an 18th century novel, and went to bed in a vile humor.

Monday . . . December 20

That title "Life Begins At Forty" is a good one to remember when looking for able men these days. There is more to it than the fact that such men are draft-free. With most men forty is the end of one cycle and the beginning of another. It is one of Nature's own periods of review and readjustment, when a man is likely to be casting about for ways to make reality come closer to his dreams. At this period even men who seem to be well set in their jobs are susceptible to suggestions for change.

Tuesday . . . December 21

One of my Washington scouts reports that the Bankhead bill is far from dead; and that its proponents have been very active among Congressmen in the past week. As soon as Congress reassembles an effort will be made to get the bill out of committee and onto the floor of the House, where the political influence of the small-town press can be used to put Congressmen on the spot. The publishers of these papers appear to have a mistaken notion that by demonstrating their great political influence they are going to prove an equally strong advertising influence. They do not seem to understand that the buying judgment of advertisers is formed in quite different ways from the political fears of Congressmen.

Wednesday . . . December 22

All products and all ideas are salable only as they flow with the tides of thought and feeling which are surging through a given society. Because the forces which create these tides are more powerful than advertising, it is futile for us to run counter to them. Thus when, as now, money has ceased to hold its normal values, economy is a weak theme. For the ad man, as for the politician, the ability to sense the rise and fall of these tides is vital; and techniques which will aid him in doing this are something he should develop as part of his standard equipment.

Thursday . . . December 23

In addition to all the *great* blessings of Peace, I am hungering for one tiny personal one. Blessed will be the day when advertisers are through with tone poems and cathedral chimes—with shooting arrows into the air that fall to earth I know not where—and

252

are willing to let my pencil get back to good, honest merchandise selling.

Friday . . . December 24

Glad to receive as a Christmas greeting a copy of "The Forgotten Man's Almanac," made up from the salty observations of that great student of society, William Graham Sumner. Sumner's whole viewpoint was the very antithesis of the New Dealers', and one of the sorriest of the many intellectual tricks indulged in by these gentlemen was the appropriation of Sumner's "Forgotten Man" phrase, and its application to the last group he ever meant it to indicate. No pseudo-scientific campaign of any advertiser ever beat that one for trickery.

Saturday . . . December 25

No matter how able a man may be financially to gratify his fancies; no matter how much he seems to have "everything"; there are always some things he won't buy for himself. These may be articles of personal adornment or indulgence, but more often they are gadgets related to a hobby. These are the things he is always hoping to find among the packages under the Christmas tree, and just one of them, irrespective of its cost, will outshine all the conventional presents. It shows that somebody has observed him closely enough, and sympathetically enough to penetrate to his secret desires. (Women's publications please copy.)

253

As another year begins its closing lines, and a new one stands off-stage, I am reminded that it is not easy to keep the past and future in perspective. In our simple ways we ad men often show it. Some who apply to me for jobs bring along huge scrapbooks of all the work they have ever done, and all the publicity they have received. These always seem to me a little like Fred Allen's backward-flying bird—not so interested in where they are going as in where they have been. Other applicants—the largest number—have to scurry about to gather up any records of their work; seeming thereby to be living just from day to day. Still others—very rare—have carefully kept case histories of ads that have worked and ads that have not; thus showing that sense of history which makes the past the instructor of the future that it ought to be.

The farmer who said he didn't need a farm paper because he already knew how to farm better than he did was speaking for all of us. The great gap between knowledge and action is the point at which advertising men often find themselves in conflict with others who would influence the public. High-minded government servants, for instance, think if they could only get enough space devoted to explaining the dangers of inflation, or the rules of good nutrition, or what not, that the job would be done.

The ad man knows that to get the *action* desired he often has to do something quite different from disseminating sound information; may, in fact, have to find his way in through the weaknesses of people rather than through their strengths. The Federal Trade Commission might well ponder this fact.

Tuesday . . . December 28

The areas in which it is hardest to get action out of human beings are those where either the rewards for action, or the punishment for failure to act, are remote. We all know that we *ought* to do such things as making a will, seeing our dentist every six months, eating a balanced diet, etc., but the pay-off, either good or bad, is too distant to spur us. In such cases one of the functions of advertising is to dramatize that postponed good or evil, as the church does Heaven and Hell, in order to rouse the sinners to action. And churchmen tell me that of the two the fires of Hell get the best results.

Wednesday . . . December 29

George Horace Lorimer, in his great days, used to say that he edited the *S.E.P.* for young men who were interested in just two things: how to get on in the world; and how to find the right girl to get on with. This week's issue seems to say, in its editorial content, that Pvt. Willie Gillis is still interested in the right girl, but that he has learned that getting on in the world involves a good deal more than the formula of the old American success story.

Thursday . . . December 30

Speaking of the *S.E.P.* reminds me of the days when its publishers used to make marked contributions to the advancement of advertising—not only by publishing basic marketing data, but by suggesting improvements in the art of visual presentation, such as the use of two colors, and layouts for two pages facing. It seems strange that no owners of printed media have carried forward work in this field, especially when auditory methods are making such competitive gains. A tithe of what the magazine publishers spend in promotion would go a long way toward uncovering new and more effective methods of transferring ideas through the eye. A compilation, alone, of what the Army has learned from its training films would be highly instructive. To make printed advertising pay the advertiser better is one good way to sell it.

Friday . . . December 31

New Year's Eve is a time for nostalgia, as I was reminded upon hearing Hildegarde sing "The Last Time I Saw Paris." There is only one line in that song which I would amend. I, too, recall that the last time I saw Paris her heart was young and gay—and no matter how she shortchanged me, I'll remember her that way.